PLANTS
OF THE
METROPLEX III

by   J. Howard Garrett

Lantana

ACKNOWLEDGEMENTS

A wonderful thing about gardeners is the great spirit of sharing information. I thank the following people who have been a great help.

Naud Burnett, Ralph Pinkus, John Dromgoole, Malcomb Beck, Beth Boettner, John Morelock, Tom Anderson, Susie Smith, Bill and Jan Neiman, Cathy Scott, Ray Entenmann, Curtis Tabor, Kevin Bassett, Peggy Hammell, Elizabeth Dodd, Kim Anderson, JoAnn Murray, David Hadden, Pete Heres, Bob McLaughlin, Marie Caillet, Kay Warnerdam, Todd Vaughn, Bill Knoop, John Thomas, Doug Prcin, Chris Corby, Carl McCord, Bonnie Thurber, Mike Hadden, Bill and Lane Furneaux, Mike Shoup, Lucille Warner, Ury Winniford, Bob Wilson, Beverly Brewer, Mark Kelley, Jack Greenberg, Ron Essman, Laura Cates, Gay and Frank Finger, Celia Fulcher, Bob Quimby, Gary Huddleston, Rick Archie, Leighton Foster, Frances Jones, Randy Weston, Allan Reed, Warren Johnson and Benny Simpson.

I also want to thank my staff for both helping with the writing and production of the book and for their work at Howard Garrett & Associates, Inc. They are Kevin Starnes, Lee Roth, Susan Klein, David Samuelson, Donna Wilkins, and Tracy Flanagan.

Copyright © 1975 by Lantana

2nd Printing 1976
3rd Printing 1978
4th Printing 1979
5th Printing 1982
6th Printing 1988
7th Printing 1989
8th Printing 1991

Library of Congress Cataloging-in-Publication Data

Garrett, J. Howard, 1947-

Plants of the Metroplex III.

Includes Index.

1. Landscaping Design   2. Gardening   3. Plant Materials

4. Landscape Installation   5. Landscape Maintenance

6. Landscape Sources   7. Environmental Issues   8. Organic Gardening

ISBN 0-9617829-00

Book Design: Howard Garrett & Associates, Inc.

Photography: Howard Garrett

Art Production and Color Work: P. Chan & Edward, Inc.
    Bob Rock, Cindy Peer

Typesetting and Camera Ready Artwork: DM Graphics

To
Judy Keag Garrett

RECOMMENDED SOURCES OF INFORMATION

- The Antique Rose Emporium, Rt. 5, Box 143G, Brenham, Texas, 77833 (409) 836-5548.

- Bio-Control Company, P.O. Box 337, Berry Creek, CA 95916 (916) 585-5227.

- Dallas Civic Garden Center, P.O. Box 26194, Dallas, Texas 75224.

- Greenhills Environmental Center, 7575 Wheatland Road, Dallas, Texas 75249.

- Garden-Ville / 6266 Hwy. 290 West, Austin, Texas 78735 / Route 3, Box 210TA, San Antonio, Texas 78218.

- Heard Natural Science Museum, Rt. 6, Box 22, McKinney, Texas 75069.

- National Wildflower Research Center, P.O. Box 1011, Austin, Texas 78767.

- Native Plant Society of Texas, P.O. Box 23836, Texas Woman's University, Denton, Texas 76204.

- Howard Garrett Pay Telephone 1-900-990-SOIL (7645).

- Pesticide Exposure, Austin, Texas 1-800-832-7347.

- *An Agricultural Testament* by Sir Albert Howard.

- *Common Sense Pest Control* by Olkowski and Daar.

- Texas Native Plant Directory of the Texas Department of Agriculture, P.O. Box 12847, Austin, Texas 78711.

- Wildflower Hotline, Marcia Coale, McKinney, Texas (214) 542-1947.

- *Landscape Design ... Texas Style* by J. Howard Garrett.

- *A Guide to Growing Herbs in North Texas* by Jacque Porter Owens.

- "Avant Gardener," Box 489, New York, NY 10028.

- *The Complete Guide to Texas Lawn Care* by Dr. William E. Knoop.

- *Classic Roses* by Peter Beale.

- *Dallas Planting Manual* by The Dallas Garden Club and The Dallas Women's Club.

- *Hortus Third* by Bailey.

- *How to Grow Native Plants of Texas and the Southwest* by Jill Nokes.

- *How to Know and Grow Texas Wildflowers* by Carroll Abbott.

- *Know It and Grow It* by Dr. Carl Whitcomb.

- *Texas Trees* by Benny Simpson.

- *Landscaping with Native Texas Plants* — Sally Wasowski and Julie Ryan.

- *Roses Love Garlic* by Louise Riotte.

- *The Louisiana Iris* by Marie Calliet and Joseph K. Mertzweiller.

- *Weeds* by Charles Walters.

- *Manual of Woody Landscape Plants* by Michael A. Dirr.

- *Seeds of Woody Plants in the United States* by the U.S. Department of Agriculture.

- *Southern Herb Growing* by Madelene Hill and Gwen Barclay.

- *Southern Plants for Landscape Design* by Neil Odenwald and James Turner.

- *Sunset Western Garden Book* by Sunset Magazine.

- *The Garden-Ville Method* by Malcomb Beck.

- *Taylor's Encyclopedia of Gardening* by Norman Taylor.

- *Texas Gardener's Guide to Growing and Using Herbs* by Diane Morey Sitton.

- "Texas Gardener Magazine" by Suntex Press.

- *Trees of North Texas* by Robert A. Vines.

- *Trees, Shrubs, and Woody Vines of the Southwest* by Robert A. Vines.

- *Silent Spring* by Rachel Carson.

- *The Vegetable Book* by Sam Cotner.

- *Wildflowers of Texas* by Geyata Ajilvsgi, Bryan, Texas, 1984.

- *The World of Irises* by The American Iris Society.

J. Howard Garrett's
ORGANIC MANUAL
Available from Lantana • P.O. Box 140650 • Dallas, Texas 75214

TABLE OF CONTENTS

FOREWORD

by Alex Burton

Before we step out into the garden let's have a definition of this term "Metroplex."

"Metroplex" is a word you won't find in your dictionary. It is a made-up word used to describe the area composed of Dallas County and Tarrant County and those eight counties that surround the other two. It is what the Census Bureau used to call "The Standard Metropolitan Statistical Area."

When Howard Garrett set out to write this book, he didn't want to restrict himself to a small area and he didn't because there are some four million people in the "Metroplex." You must not think that because you live outside it that this book is not for you. It is for you; you *and* your garden.

The first settlers to Texas from the United States were impressed with the trees, and the vines, and the flowers.

Modern day visitors to this part of Texas are impressed with the variety of trees and shrubs and flowers and things that can be seen growing and flowering on every hand.

The first time gardener here in the Metroplex is impressed, if not overwhelmed, when faced with the broad choices of what to grow in the garden. Make no mistake those who have homes here want to have as many trees and shrubs and flowering vines as they can squeeze onto the property and that's why this book is so valuable. It will save the home gardener, or the professional for that matter, money in the long run because Howard Garrett has tried to teach us restraint in these pages.

Howard provides the information of what a plant or tree will look like and how much space it will occupy when it is fully grown. He explains not only the necessity of planning ahead but how to do it.

This book is going to save you time as well because you will note that Howard favors the natural system all the way through. He doesn't like a phony or forced design and he favors natural systems of insect and disease control. The book you are holding in your hand is a sensible book written by a sensible man. He's made all the mistakes in the past. If you follow his directions now you won't be making those same mistakes.

A garden should be a reward: the reward of planning, the reward of preparation, the reward of having a beautiful place in which to relax and this is a relaxing book. Time after time you are going to see the suggestion to let nature handle the growing. It's good advice.

I know you are going to have a good garden because you've taken the first important step. You've bought this book!

Alex. M. A. Burton

Dallas, Texas
August 4, 1988

COMMITMENT TO THE ENVIRONMENT

Plants of the Metroplex started in 1974 when I discovered that no book existed showing the plants I was teaching about and designing into projects. I completed the original book in one year because business was so bad in Dallas that year I had plenty of free time.

Since then my love of plants has grown substantially, along with my understanding and appreciation of the world of ornamental horticulture.

Although I didn't realize it in the beginning, my plant material recommendations have always included a high percentage of native plants — I just didn't identify them as such. Now that interest and use of natives has increased, 50 additional native plants and 170 introduced plants have been added to the book. I strongly believe that certain introduced plants are excellent and some even superior to their native counterparts. Using a careful mixture of both native and introduced plants is sensible in most gardens.

Environmental issues are a major concern

today and a more organic approach to landscape design and gardening is in order. The health and well being of your family is at stake. Organic gardening is no longer a fad. We gardeners put far too many chemicals and poisons into our environment. Not only are we polluting the world, but we are killing ourselves in the process. Listen to the radio talk shows on gardening; every other question has an answer of some poison spray, fungicide, insecticide, herbicide or stump killer. I have become painfully aware of the problem in trying to decide how to control the insect and disease problems in my own garden. I have been delighted to discover that the natural alternatives really work.

Another scary issue is how much we are poisoning the environment with fertilizers. First of all, most inorganic fertilizers have a salt base which is a problem for the already alkaline soils in most of Texas. Secondly, these fertilizers are causing a toxic build up of nitrates in the soil and drinking water. Farmers are now aware of the problem and are looking

to alternative methods and products — we home gardeners should be doing the same. And finally, chemical fertilizers destroy the beneficial microorganisms in the soil. More on that later.

Plants of the Metroplex III covers the proper selection and use of plant materials in the North Texas area, including planting design, installation and maintenance.

Three kinds of plants are shown and discussed: 1) recommended plants 2) plants that can be used but aren't highly recommended and 3) plants that are not recommended and should not be planted. I am not noncommittal about the plants in this book. My likes, dislikes and experiences with all the plants are clearly expressed. The simple identification of the various plants isn't really worth much. What I hope you receive of value here results from the editorial pros and cons based on my experience with all the **400** plus plants. Although no plant or technique is perfect, I have tried to give you the best advice on how to achieve the greatest success with a new or renovated garden.

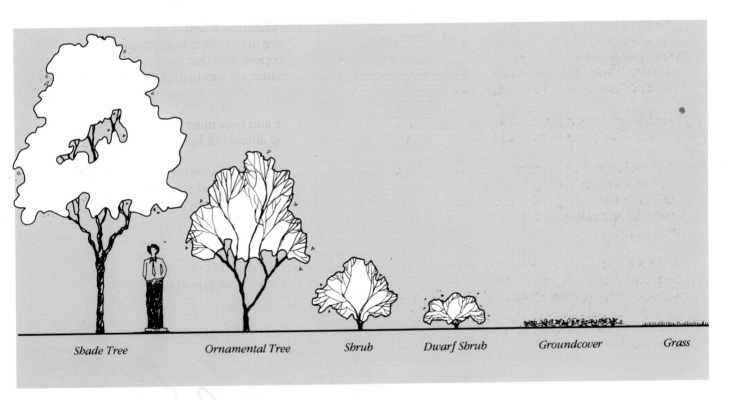

| Shade Tree | Ornamental Tree | Shrub | Dwarf Shrub | Groundcover | Grass |

PLANTING DESIGN

Creating successful landscaping is not difficult if certain basic steps are taken: 1) Careful selection of native and well-adapted plant types 2) Organic bed preparation 3) Drainage solutions 4) Organic planting techniques 5) Organic maintenance procedures. By achieving the first four steps, maintenance will be easy and enjoyable.

Landscape gardens are never static. They are dynamic and continue to change with age. One of the great pleasures of gardening is to

fine tune the landscaping by moving plants about, adding plants when needed and removing those that are no longer useful.

A garden has at least two lives — the first when it is installed, the second when the trees mature and shade the ground. When the trees are young, the majority of the shrubs, ground covers and grasses must be those that thrive in the full sun. Later as the trees grow and mature, the situation changes. Shade becomes the order of the day and the low plants and understory trees must be shade tolerant.

> Gardens should be allowed to change over time — they're going to anyway!

TREES

Trees are the first consideration. Statistics show that landscaping is the only home improvement that can return up to 200% of the original investment. I think the most important single element of that investment is the trees. In addition to adding beauty, trees create the atmosphere or feel of a garden. They invite us, shade us, surprise us, house wildlife, create backgrounds and niches, inspire and humble us. Trees increase in value as they grow and save energy and money by shading our houses in the summer and by letting the sun shine through for warmth in the winter.

Choosing the correct tree for the correct spot is not just an aesthetic decision, but an important investment decision as well. The critical consideration in selecting a tree for a particular site is not how pretty you think the tree will look growing in that particular spot, but rather how the tree will like that particular spot. Understanding the horticultural needs of a tree is essential.

There are two categories of trees: shade and ornamental. Shade trees are the large structural trees that form the skeleton of the planting plan and grow to be 40' to 100' tall. They are used to create the outdoor spaces, block undesirable views and provide shade. This category includes the Oaks, Elms, Pecans and other long-lived trees.

> Trees, if used properly and not simply scattered out all over the site, function as the walls and roofs of our outdoor rooms.

Of all the plants, shade trees provide the greatest long-term value, so their use should be carefully considered and given a large percentage of the landscape budget.

Ornamental trees are those used for aesthetics, to create focal points and grow to be 8' to 30' tall. Trees such as Crabapple, Hawthorn, Crape Myrtle are used primarily for their spring or summer flower color. Others, such as Yaupon or Wax Myrtle, are used for their evergreen color or berries. Some, such as Japanese Maple, are used for their distinctive foliage color and interesting branching characteristics.

SHRUBS

Shrubs should be selected on the basis of what variety will grow best in the space provided. If more than one variety will work, this decision becomes subjective based on the desire for flowers, interesting foliage, fall

color, etc. However, horticultural requirements should be the prerequisite and have priority over aesthetic considerations. Tall-growing varieties are used for background plantings and screens. Medium-height shrubs are used for flower display or evergreen color. Dwarf varieties are used for masses and interesting bed shapes.

GROUND COVER

Ground cover plants are low-growing, viney and grasslike materials that are primarily used to cover large areas of ground. They are best used where grass won't grow and for creating interesting bed shapes. Ground covers are usually the best choice in heavily shady areas. Often the ground covers become the last phase of the permanent garden installation and are planted after the trees have matured to shade the ground.

VINES

Vines are usually fast-growing plants that twine or cling to climb vertically on walls, fences, posts or overhead structures. They are used for quick shade, vertical softening or colorful flower display. Vines are an inexpensive way to have lots of greenery and color in a hurry. They are also quite good in smaller spaces where wide-growing shrubs and trees would be a problem.

HERBS

Herbs or "erbs" as some like to call them make wonderful landscape plants and should be used more in ornamental gardens even if gourmet cooking is not in the plans. The traditional definition of a herb is a herbaceous plant that is used to flavor foods, provide medicinal properties or offer up fragrances. Herbs fall into several categories; shrubs, ground covers, annuals and perennials and are therefore distributed throughout the pages of this book.

> Shade gardens are the easiest to maintain — less watering and fewer weeds to fight.

FLOWERS

Flowers are an important finishing touch to any fine garden. Everyone loves flowers. Annuals are useful for that dramatic splash of one-season color and the perennials are valuable because of their faithful return to bloom year after year. Since replacing annual color each year is expensive, annuals should be concentrated to one or a few spots rather than scattering them all about. The perennial flowers can be used more randomly throughout the garden.

> Natives and introduced plants can and should be used together. Biodiversity is an important aspect of proper design and proper horticulture.

GRASSES

Grasses should be selected on horticultural requirements. For example, large sunny areas that will have active use should use Common Bermudagrass or Buffalograss. Shady, less-used areas should use St. Augustine. Areas that will not have much water should use Buffalograss. Areas that need a smooth, highly refined surface should use the hybrid Tifgrasses.

DESIGN MISTAKES

Some of the worst planting mistakes I see on both residential and commercial properties are:
1. Choosing plants that require too much care.
2. Choosing plants that cannot grow in our soil.
3. Failure to allow for proper drainage.
4. Failure to mulch bare soil.
5. Planting too many plants of the same type.
6. Assuming that native plants are maintenance-free and need no supplemental water or care for establishment.

SPECIAL NOTE:

Many poisonous plants exist. Children need to be taught which ones can be eaten and which are dangerous. It is best not to let them eat any plants without your approval and supervision.

LANDSCAPE INSTALLATION

Soils

The first and most important hard material is the soil itself. Landscape gardens have one or a combination of soil types; clay, silt, loam, sandy loam, sand, gravel and rock. Clay soils have the smallest particles, compact the most and drain the least. Sand, gravel and broken rock have the largest particles, compact the least and drain the best. Soil contains five major components: Organic material, minerals, water, air and living organisms. The living

organisms are very important and consist of worms, insects, plants, algae, bacteria, fungi and other microorganisms.

Loose, organic, well-drained soils are best. Tightly structured clays of North Texas are nutritious soils, but need to be loosened to improve drainage and allow oxygen into the root zone. North Texas soils also need large quantities of organic matter. The presence of microorganisms is also very important.

> The first six inches of soil is where most roots reside and is a living and constantly changing environment.

Healthy soils must also have a balance of minerals. A soil test is needed to monitor the percentage of the mineral nutrients. A balanced soil should have approximately the following percentages of available nutrients:

68% calcium, 12% magnesium, 5% potassium and adequate amounts of all the other mineral elements including sulfur, iron, copper, zinc, molybdenum, boron and manganese. If the mineral balance of the soil is correct, the pH will be between 6.3 and 6.8. A pH of 7.0 is neutral.

Soil Amendments

Soil amendments are those materials that improve the structure and chemical makeup of the soil. In general, soil that is too acid with pH lower than 6.2 can be modified with lime (limestone) and soil that is too alkaline with pH higher than 6.5 can be modified with sulfur or organic materials. Other soil amendments are also available for various specific purposes.

- **Sulfur** is a needed amendment if your soil is too high in calcium, which most North Texas soils are. If calcium is too high, magnesium will usually be too low and most of the trace minerals will be tied up and unavailable to plants.

- **Organic matter** helps balance the chemical and physical nature of the soil. The best organic matter for bed preparation is compost. Compost can be made from anything that was once alive. Organic matter provides humus and aids in the loosening of the soil by adding larger particles than the soil particles and by providing food for microorganisms.

> 85 percent of a plant's roots are found in the first six inches of soil. Therefore there's no need to work organic material into the soil very deeply.

My least favorite organic matter for bed preparation is peat moss because it is too far decomposed to last long, is the most expensive organic material, and must be purchased from sources that are several hundred miles outside Texas. An environmental consideration also exists related to the harvesting of peat moss from bogs.

> DRAINAGE
> A plant's health depends on the soil's ability to drain away excess water. If water fills the pores in the soil, there is no room for oxygen.

- **Fertilizers** are available in two forms: organic and synthetic. Organic fertilizers are the products of decayed plants and animals. They contain smaller amounts of N-P-K than do synthetic fertilizers, but they can contain all the trace minerals that are needed by plants — that's because they come from plants. Organic fertilizers all have natural slow release and provide humus for the soil. Synthetic fertilizers are manmade chemical fertilizers, usually water-soluble and high in N-P-K percentages.

Nitrogen produces green color and foliage growth. It is also the element that can seriously burn plants, so be careful with nitrogen fertilizers. **Phosphorous** aids the movement and storage of energy in the plant, helps root development, and contributes to the health of the other plant parts. For instance, phosphorous helps create more abundant and larger blooms. **Potassium** (Potash) is essential to the balance between leaf and root growth, and is necessary for winter and summer hardiness. This element exists in great quantities in the soil of North Texas area but is mostly tied up in the soil and unavailable to plants.

Plants depend on three other essential nutrients derived from air and water: carbon, hydrogen, and oxygen. Plants also depend on nutrients derived from the minerals in the form of inorganic salts - iron, calcium, magnesium, sulfur, manganese, chlorine, boron, zinc, copper, and molybdenum. The other seventy or so trace minerals are not fully understood but are important to the soil and to Nature's whole.

When fertilizing and adding mineral nutrients, it's important to think about balance. Healthy soils and plants have a balance of elements and ingredients. A proper fertilization program will help keep the balance intact. That's why it's important to avoid an overkill of the well-known elements nitrogen, phosphorous and potassium, better known as N-P-K.

Here's a good example. The following are the percentages of various elements in whole plants:

- Oxygen   45 percent
- Carbon   44 percent
- Hydrogen   6 percent
- Nitrogen   2 percent
- Potassium   1.1 percent
- Phosphorous   0.4 percent
- Sulfur   0.5 percent
- Calcium   0.6 percent
- Magnesium   0.3 percent

Note the relatively low percentages of nitrogen, phosphorous and potassium and the high percentages of oxygen, carbon and hydrogen. When buying fertilizer, remember how relatively unimportant nitrogen, phosphorous and potassium are. Think in terms of providing the soil those products and elements that will help maintain the natural balance. If the soil is in a healthy, balanced condition (which includes organic matter and air), nitrogen, potassium and phosphorous will be produced naturally by the feeding of microorganisms and relatively little will need to be added.

Mulches

Organic materials also have another important function — as mulch. Mulches are used to cover the bare soil after planting has been done. My favorites are coarse-shredded hardwood bark for annuals and perennials and alfalfa hay for roses and vegetables. Other available mulches include grain straw, pine needles, decomposed sawdust, cotton seed hulls, pecan hulls and wood chips.

> Organic mulch keeps the soil cool during hot summer months, prevents weed growth, and slows the evaporation of moisture from the soil.

I don't like plastics, fabrics or gravel. They are much harder on the plants and are unattractive. They also don't break down into humus for the soil. Pine bark is my least favorite organic mulch because its flat pieces are easily washed or blown away.

SOIL PREPARATION AND PLANTING

In general, the ideal time to plant trees, shrubs and spring-blooming perennials is fall; second best is anytime in the winter; third is the spring; last is in the heat of summer. Planting in the fall or winter offers roots a chance to start growing before the foliage emerges in the spring.

Most plants can be planted any month of the year if the following precautions are taken:

- **Hot part of summer** — When transporting plants in an open vehicle, cover to protect the foliage from the sun and wind and keep the root ball moist. Always dampen the planting beds prior to planting.

- **Freezing weather** — Don't leave plants out of the ground during extreme cold without protecting the roots from possible freeze damage. Store plants in sunny areas prior to planting. Always keep the plants moist and mulched during freezing weather. Once in the ground, plants will normally survive a freeze.

- **Mild weather** — The mild weather can make you forget to keep containers or newly planted material moist, so check often but do not overwater.

Trees

Trees are by far the most important landscape element. They create the garden space and are the skeleton or framework for all else that happens. They are also the only landscape element that appreciates greatly in value through the years.

There's only one catch. If the trees aren't healthy and don't grow, they won't do you any good at all. To grow properly, trees must be planted properly. Many tree planting procedures are not only horticulturally incorrect, but are substantial wastes of money. My recommendations for tree planting have developed over years of carefully studying many planting techniques and trying to understand what works and what doesn't.

The very first trees I saw planted correctly occurred in 1976. I had been commissioned to design the landscaping for the Harris Corporation on Dallas North Parkway in Addison, Texas. The budget was tight and the site was large and uninteresting.

Utilizing the excess soil from the building excavation, free-flowing berms were created to add interest and provide sites for trees to be planted. I didn't realize at the time the importance of the built-in drainage system the berms provided.

An old friend, Cody Carter, planted all the trees on that job. Since that time, I've watched those trees and I've watched trees on other projects planted using all kinds of various techniques. Here's what I learned and recommend.

1. DIG AN UGLY HOLE

The hole should be dug exactly the same depth as the height of the ball. Don't guess — actually measure the height of the ball. Never plant trees in slick-sided or glazed holes such as those caused by a tree spade or auger. Holes with glazed sides greatly restrict root penetration into the surrounding soil and consequently limit proper root development.

2. RUN A PERK TEST

Simply fill the hole with water and wait until the next day. If the water level doesn't drop substantially overnight (at least 5 or 6 inches), a drainage problem is indicated. At this point, the tree needs to be moved to another location or have drainage added in the form of a PVC drainline set in gravel running from the hole to a lower point on the site. Another draining method that sometimes works is a pier hole dug down from the bottom of the hole into a different soil type and filled with gravel. A sump from the top of the ball down to the bottom of the ball does little if any good. Positive drainage is critical so don't shortcut this step.

3. BACKFILL WITH EXISTING SOIL

Place the tree in the center of the hole, making sure that the top of the ball is perfectly flush with surrounding grade. Backfill with the soil that came from the hole. This is a critical point. Do not add sand, foreign soil, organic matter or fertilizer into the backfill. The roots need to start growing in the native soil from the beginning. When the hole is dug in solid rock, topsoil from the same area should be used. Some native rock mixed into the backfill is beneficial.

Water the backfill very carefully making, sure to get rid of all air pockets. Adding amendments to the backfill such as peat moss, sand, or foreign soils not only wastes money but is detrimental to the tree. Putting gravel in the bottom of the hole is a total waste of money.

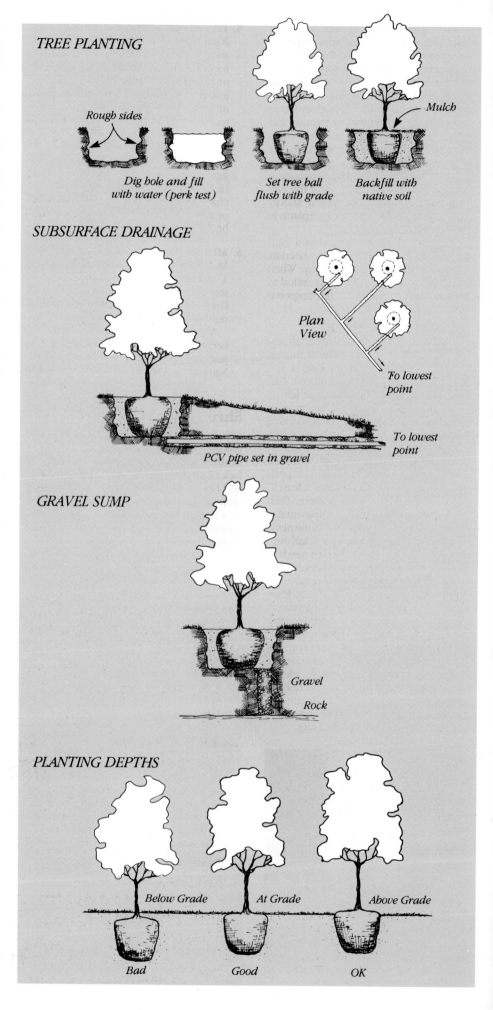

TREE PLANTING

Rough sides

Dig hole and fill with water (perk test)

Set tree ball flush with grade

Backfill with native soil

Mulch

SUBSURFACE DRAINAGE

Plan View

To lowest point

To lowest point

PCV pipe set in gravel

GRAVEL SUMP

Gravel

Rock

PLANTING DEPTHS

Below Grade

At Grade

Above Grade

Bad

Good

OK

When planting balled and burlapped plants, leave burlap on the sides of the ball after planting but loosen at the trunk and remove the burlap from the top of the ball. Remove any nylon or plastic covering or string, since these materials do not decompose and can girdle the truck and roots as the plant grows. Studies have shown that even wire mesh should be removed to avoid root girdling because wire does not break down very fast in our alkaline soils.

When planting from plastic containers, carefully remove plants and tear the outside roots if they have grown solidly against the container. Never leave plants in containers.

Bare-rooted plants, balled and burlapped, and container plant materials should be planted the same way. When planting bare-rooted plants, it is critical to keep the roots moist during the transportation and planting process.

4. DO NOT WRAP OR STAKE

Trunks of newly planted trees should not be wrapped. It's a waste of money, looks unattractive, harbors insects and leaves the bark weak when removed. Tree wrapping is similar to a bandage left on your finger too long. If you are worried about the unlikely possibility of sunburn, it's much better to paint the trunk with a diluted white latex paint.

Staking and guying is usually unnecessary if the tree has been planted properly with the proper earth ball size of at least 9" of ball for each 1" of trunk diameter. Staking is a waste of money and detrimental to the proper trunk development of the plant. In rare circumstances (sandy soil, tall evergreen trees, etc.) where the tree needs to be staked for a while, use the simple technique shown in the photo and remove the stakes as soon as possible. Never leave them on more than one growing season. Temporary staking should be done with strong wire, metal or wooden stakes and pieces of garden hose at the tree to prevent injury. Staking should only be done as a last resort — it is unsightly, expensive, adds to mowing and trimming costs and restricts the tree's ability to develop tensile strength in the trunk. It can also cause damage to the cambium layer. Remove all tags.

Tree staking

5. DO NOT OVERPRUNE

It's an old wives' tale that limb pruning must be done to compensate for the loss of roots during transplanting or planting. Most trees fare much better if all the limbs and foliage are left intact. The more foliage, the more food can be produced to build the root system. The health of the root system is the key to the overall health of the tree.

The only trees that seem to respond positively to thinning at the time of transplanting are field-collected Live Oak, Yaupon Holly and other evergreens. Plants purchased in containers definitely need no pruning and deciduous trees don't need to be thinned.

6. MULCH THE TOP OF BALL

Mulch the top of the ball after planting with 1" of compost and then 3" of mulch. This step is important in lawn areas or in beds. Don't ever plant grass over the tree ball until the tree has established.

If my recommendations sound easy, it is because they are. Much can be learned by just paying close attention to Mother Nature's methods.

Shrubs, Ground Covers, Vines

Soil preparation is necessary for all shrubs, ground covers and vines. Most of the soils in North Texas have two basic problems: (1) lack of humus and related biological activity and (2) density of the soil particles, causing drainage problems and lack of oxygen in the root zone. In order to help overcome these problems, the following soil preparations are recommended:

- Excavate beds to a depth necessary to remove all weeds and grass, including rhizomes (underground stems). No excavation should be done in bare soil areas.
- If needed, add topsoil to all beds to within 2" of the adjacent finished grade. Use native topsoil, similar to that topsoil which is on the site. I do not recommend using herbicides to kill grass and weeds prior to excavation.
- Cover areas to be planted with a 4"-6" depth of compost and apply a 100% organic fertilizer at the rate of 10 lbs. per 1,000 sq. ft.
- Till the compost and the existing topsoil together to a depth of 6"-8".
- After thoroughly tilling all beds, rake smooth all areas to eliminate undulations.
- The top of the beds should be flat and higher than surrounding grade with sloped edges and a slight ditch at the edge of the bed for drainage.
- Soil tests are helpful to show you the current condition of the soil. Be sure to use a testing lab that bases its analysis on the cation exchange capacity (CEC) and always order the micronutrient tests. Soil tests that only check for N-P-K are worthless.

Planting beds should be moistened before planting begins. Do not plant in dry soil! Shrubs and vines should be planted from 1,2,3,5 or 7 gallon containers in prepared beds and backfilled with the improved bed preparation soil. Plants should be watered by sticking the hose down beside the ball and soaking thoroughly.

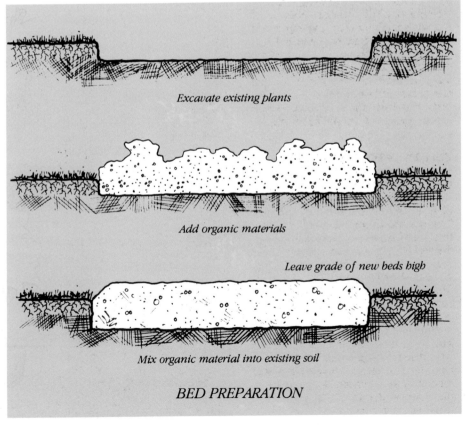

Excavate existing plants

Add organic materials

Leave grade of new beds high

Mix organic material into existing soil

BED PREPARATION

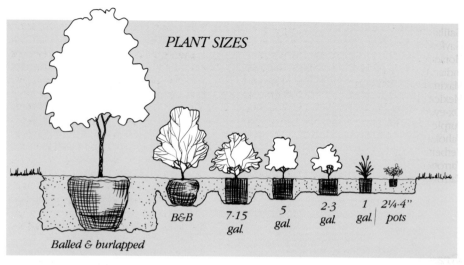

PLANT SIZES

Balled & burlapped *B&B* *7-15 gal.* *5 gal.* *2-3 gal.* *1 gal.* *2¼-4" pots*

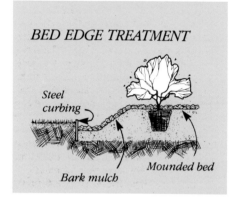

BED EDGE TREATMENT

Steel curbing

Bark mulch

Mounded bed

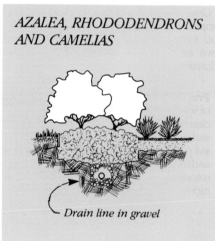

AZALEA, RHODODENDRONS AND CAMELIAS

Drain line in gravel

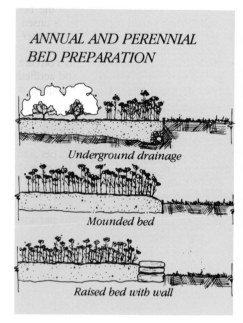

ANNUAL AND PERENNIAL BED PREPARATION

Underground drainage

Mounded bed

Raised bed with wall

Ground covers should be planted from 2¼", 4" pots or 1 gallon containers. It is extremely important to dampen the soil prior to planting. In the hot months, this will greatly reduce plant losses. Consistent watering and mulching are also critical during the establishment period (1st growing season). These small plants should only be planted in well-prepared beds.

Azaleas, Camellias and Rhododendrons

These are acid-loving plants and our soil certainly isn't that. Here's what to do if you insist on trying to grow these high-maintenance plants:

- Excavate and remove existing soil to a depth of 4". The width of the bed should be at least 24" for each row of plants.
- Backfill with a mixture of 50% compost, 50% shredded hardwood bark, copperas @ 2 lb./cubic yard and granulated sulfur @ 1 lb./cubic yard. Place in the bed area to a depth of 16". Be sure to thoroughly saturate this mixture in a tub or wheelbarrow prior to placing it in the bed.
- Mound the beds so that the finished grade is about 12" above the adjacent grade.
- Tear or cut the pot-bound roots before planting. This is very important, for without this step, the roots will never break away from the ball and the plant often dies.
- **Note:** If you live in an acid soil area, simply add 8" of quality compost and correct the mineral deficiencies that show up on the soil test.

Annuals and Perennials

Flower beds should be built the same as shrub and ground cover beds with the addition of 2 more inches of organic material. These beds should also be mounded or raised more than other plant beds if possible. Raised flower beds are critical for proper drainage.

- **Flowers** (Annuals & Perennials) are often planted in the same beds as the shrubs and ground covers. Some annuals and perennials can tolerate this, but gardeners would have greater success with their flowers if they would do one simple thing — raise or mound the flower beds. Flower beds can simply be mounded 6 to 9 inches by adding compost. Mixing at least some of the existing soil into the concoction is a good idea.

- **Bulbs** should always be planted in prepared beds. Bulbs will do better with a tablespoon of bone meal or colloidal phosphate cultivated into the bottom of the hole. Earthworm castings are an excellent addition to each bulb hole and the plants will be larger and more showy if soaked in a 1% solution of Agrispon or other stimulator prior to planting.

Transplanting

Established plants should be relocated only during the dormant periods — usually in the fall or winter. The larger the plant, the more difficult the transplant. Smaller plants that have not developed an extensive root system can be moved during the growing season if watered-in immediately. Transplanted plants, should be installed with the same techniques used for new plants as explained previously.

Mulching

Mulching should be done after planting is completed. Acceptable mulches are shredded hardwood bark, pine needles, coarse compost, pecan shells or shredded cypress bark. Mulch should be at least 2" deep on top of planting beds, 3"-4" is better. Mulching helps hold moisture in the beds, controls weeds and keeps the soil temperature at 84° plus or minus.

Do not use plastic sheets as a mulch. The plant's root system will cook from the heat buildup. Plastic also cuts off the oxygen needed by the soil. I also do not recommend fabrics or gravel as mulches. Nothing compares to a thick layer of organic material.

Weed Control

Weed control is best done by hand and by mulching heavily. It's important to understand that a few weeds are not a big deal. Good cultural practices and healthy soil will eliminate most noxious weed problems.

Wildflowers

In the past, much of the wildflower planting was done by scattering the seed out over bare ground and hoping something would come up. As a result, few gardeners were having success with wildflowers. The proper method for growing wildflowers is as follows:

- Remove all weeds and loosen any heavily compacted areas. No need to remove rock. A light rototilling (1" deep) is the best bed preparation.
- Soil amendments and fertilizers are not needed other than a light application (5 pounds per 1000 square feet) of 100% organic fertilizer.
- Treat the seed prior to planting with a 1% solution of Agrispon, Bioform or Medina.
- Apply the seed at the recommended rate, making sure to get good soil/seed contact and lightly rake the seed into the soil. Spring-blooming wildflowers should be planted the previous September in order to take advantage of the fall rains.
- Apply supplemental watering in the fall and in the spring if the weather is unseasonably dry. If rains are normal, no watering is needed.
- It is best to plant wildflowers either on bare ground or in heavily scalped and aerified Buffalo or Bermudagrass. Buffalograss is best.

WILDFLOWER SEEDING RATES

Black-eyed Susan	3 lb. per acre
Bluebonnet	30 lb. per acre
Butterfly Weed	10 lb. per acre
Coreopsis	10 lb. per acre
Crimson Clover	15 lb. per acre
Englemann Daisy	5 lb. per acre
Evening Primrose	½ lb. per acre
Gaillardia	10 lb. per acre
Gayfeather	10 lb. per acre
Horsemint	3 lb. per acre
Indian Paintbrush	¼ lb. per acre
Maximillian Sunflower	2 lb. per acre
Mexican Hat	2 lb. per acre
Ox-eyed Daisy	5 lb. per acre
Purple Coneflower	12 lb. per acre
Tahoka Daisy	5 lb. per acre
Verbena	6 lb. per acre
Yarrow (gold)	½ lb. per acre
Yarrow (white)	1½ lb. per acre

Grasses

Grass planting techniques can be quite simple or waste huge amounts of money. If you follow these simple techniques, your lawn establishment can be enjoyable and affordable.

- **Preparation** should include the removal of weed tops, debris, and rocks over 2" in diameter from the surface. Rocks within the soil are no problem because they actually aid positive drainage. Till to a depth of 1" and rake topsoil into a smooth grade. Deep rototilling is unnecessary and a waste of money unless the soil is heavily compacted.

Although the introduction of some organic material can be beneficial, soil amendments are usually unnecessary and only on solid rock areas is the addition of native topsoil needed. Imported topsoil is a waste of money and can cause a perched (trapped) water table and lawn problems.

Sloped areas should have an erosion protection material such as jute mesh, placed on the soil prior to planting. Follow the manufacturer's recommendation for installation.

Some people recommend and use herbicides to kill weeds prior to planting. I don't! These chemicals are extremely hazardous and damaging to the soil biology.

- **Seeding and Hydromulching** should be done so that the seed is in direct contact with the soil. The seed should be placed on the bare soil first and the hydromulch blown on top of the seed. One of the worst mistakes I see in grass planting is mixing the seed in the hydromulch. This causes the seed to germinate in the mulch, suspended above the soil, and many of the seeds are lost from drying out.

Night temperatures must be 65° - 70° for Bermudagrass or Buffalograss germination and no lower than 40° in the fall and winter for Fescue or other cool season grasses.

After spreading the seed, thoroughly

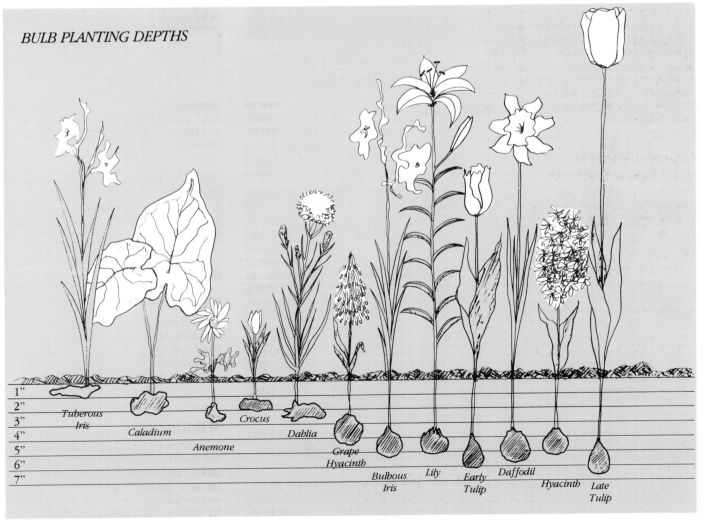

BULB PLANTING DEPTHS

Tuberous Iris — Caladium — Anemone — Crocus — Dahlia — Grape Hyacinth — Bulbous Iris — Lily — Early Tulip — Daffodil — Hyacinth — Late Tulip

soak the ground and lightly water the seeded area 2-4 times per day. Fertilize with a 100% organic fertilizer sometime before the first mowing. As the seed germinates, watch for bare spots. Reseed these bare areas immediately. Continue the light watering until the grass has solidly covered the area. At this time, begin the regular watering and maintenance program.

- **Spot sodding** is done by planting 4" x 4" squares flush with the existing grade, 12" to 18" on center. Grading, smoothing and leveling of the area to be grassed is important. Organic fertilizer should be applied after planting at the rate of 10 lbs. per 1,000 sq. ft. Regular maintenance and watering should be started at this time. This is not a planting procedure I recommend, because it is slow to cover, and often results in an uneven lawn.

- **Solid sod blocks** should be laid joint to joint after first fertilizing the ground with a 100% organic fertilizer at the rate of 20 lbs.

per 1,000 sq. ft. Grading, leveling, and smoothing prior to planting is very important. The joints between the blocks of sod can be filled with compost to give an even more finished look to the lawn.

- **Tifgrasses** (Tifway 419, Tifgreen 328, and Tifdwarf) are dwarf forms of Common Bermudagrass. They should be planted by solid sodding or hydromulching sprigs with the same procedures as used for Bermudagrass. Tifgrasses are sterile hybrids and expensive to maintain. I do not recommend these grasses for homeowners.

- **Cool season grasses** such as Fescue, Ryegrass, Bentgrass and Bluegrass (Poa trivialis) should be planted in September, October or anytime during the winter when the temperature is above 40°. Seeding rates are shown below. In all cases, the newly-applied seed should be watered at least 2 times daily until the grass has grown to the point of covering the ground.

RATES OF SEED APPLICATION

Bermudagrass	2 lbs. per 1,000 sq. ft.
Fescue	10 lbs. per 1,000 sq. ft.
Ryegrass	10 lbs. per 1,000 sq. ft.
Bentgrass	2 lbs. per 1,000 sq. ft.
Buffalograss	5 lbs. per 1,000 sq. ft.
St. Augustine	Plant solid or spot sod
Zoysia	Plant solid sod only
Tifgrass	5 sprigs per sq. foot or solid sod

INSTALLATION MISTAKES

Some of the worst installation mistakes I see on both residential and commercial projects are:
1. Failure to mulch beds.
2. Planting plants (especially trees) too low.
3. Failure to provide proper drainage.
4. Planting in smooth or glazed-wall holes.
5. Planting the wrong kind of red oaks.
6. Staking and wrapping trees unnecessarily.
7. Mixing seed into the hydromulch mix.

LANDSCAPE MAINTENANCE

Gardens are designed every day that look great on paper and look good when first planted but look pretty awful two years later.

It has been said that poorly designed gardens can be successful if maintained well. Conversely, well-designed gardens which are poorly maintained are usually failures. The design of any garden, large or small, must include maintenance considerations in the early planning stages.

Unlike buildings or structures which look their best the day they are finished, gardens should look good when finished but improve each year. Landscaping, as opposed to architecture, is never static. Gardens are complex living organisms which not only change seasonally, but also grow and mature through time. The resulting change from the time of installation to later years is quite significant.

The best maintenance program is one that is as natural as possible.

> **MAINTAINING THE FOREST FLOOR**
> Add about 1" of compost and 3" of mulch to all planting beds every year. Most soil structure and nutrition problems can be solved with good organic matter. Clippings will provide the organic matter for lawn areas.

TREES
Protection of Existing Trees

Maintenance and protection of existing trees in Texas should be greatly improved. Staying away from the root system and leaving the grade and the drainage pattern (both surface and underground) intact are essential to a tree's health. Although a tree's roots grow out far beyond the drip line of the foliage, protecting the area from the drip line to trunk

will give trees a pretty good chance to live. Installing a physical barrier such as a wire or wood fence is the only method that works to keep automobile and foot traffic, fill soil and construction debris off the root system. Since buying new trees is expensive, I recommend you work hard to keep any existing ones alive.

Pruning

In general, people prune too much. I will admit that some trees require more pruning than others. For example, Live Oaks require more regular pruning than any tree, whereas Bur Oak and Chinese Pistachio require almost no pruning.

Many trees are too drastically thinned, artificially lifted, or severely cut back. A good rule of thumb for trimming trees is to try to copy Mother Nature's pruning techniques. Pruning a tree into an artificial shape is a waste of money, has ugly results and is usually detrimental to the health of the plant. If you can't decide whether to trim or not, don't!

A common mistake is lifting or raising the bottom of the plant by removal of lower limbs. The lower limbs add to the grace and beauty of the tree and the excessive removal of lower limbs can cause stress and lead to other health related problems. This procedure doesn't necessarily allow more light to the grass or other planting beneath. If the top of the tree has not been thinned, a solid canopy still exists and no significant increase of light to the ground plane has been created. It's best to remove only dead or damaged limbs, limbs that are rubbing, limbs with mistletoe or disease and, in certain cases, enough of the canopy to allow shafts of sunlight all the way through the tree to the ground below.

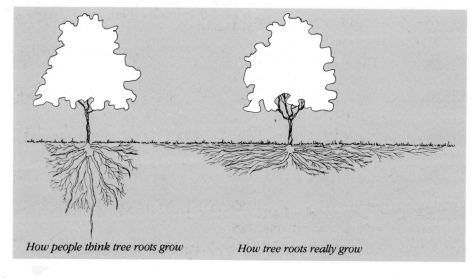

How people think tree roots grow   *How tree roots really grow*

Improper tree pruning cut

Proper tree pruning cut

Pruning cuts should never be made flush to the tree trunk. A small stub, the branch collar, should be preserved because it is the part of the tree which provides the natural healing process for the cut.

Pruning paint should **not** be used. Damage to living tissue will always heal faster if exposed to fresh air. Pruning paint can seal moisture and disease spores into a protected environment and actually increase the spread of problems.

Cabling is another very expensive technique which in most cases is unnecessary and detrimental to the tree. Cabling simply moves the stress point from one position to another. Cables are unsightly and create an artificial tension in the tree that can actually lead to more ice breakage instead of less. The only time cabling should be used is to keep a weak crotch from splitting.

Aerifying

Mechanical aeration of the root systems of trees is done while aerating the lawn or planting beds under the trees.

Mulching

Trees should be mulched at the time of planting and at least for the first growing season. Place a 3"-4" layer of mulch over the root ball of the tree to prevent the competition of grass roots. If trees are planted in beds, the entire bed should be mulched.

Fertilizing

The rate or fertilizer should be based on the surface area to be fertilized, rather than the caliper inches of the tree trunk. Organic programs feed the soil rather the plants so the amount of fertilizer is related to the amount of area, not the number or kind of plants.

I normally fertilize once in the early spring and again in early summer with a 100% organic fertilizer such as GreenSense or Sustane at the rate of 20 lb/1000 sq. ft. A third application is sometimes needed in the fall. Fertilizer should be spread on the surface of the soil rather than put in holes around the trees. The root system of trees is much more shallow than most people realize, at least 85% or the roots are located in the top 12"-18" of soil.

Earthworms are Mother Nature's tillers and soil conditioners. Besides integrating organic material into the soil, earthworms manufacture great fertilizer. One reason for using natural fertilizers in your garden is that they encourage native earthworms.

Natural fertilizers have many trace elements and, in general, last longer than chemical fertilizers and do not have to be used as often. Homemade compost is the best.

Watering

Watering is the most variable function in the maintenance puzzle due to variable soils, climates, plant materials and plant exposure to sun or shade.

If trees are planted properly in the beginning, very little extra watering is needed except during the heat of the summer. The idea is to keep the ground at a relatively even

ORGANIC FERTILIZERS AND SOIL AMENDMENTS

	N	P	K	
Alfalfa	3%	1%	2%	Vitamin A, folic acid, trace elements, enzymes, "triacontanol".
Bat Guano	10	3	1	Excellent phosphorus and trace element fertilizer.
Bioform	4	2	4	Liquid fish emulsion, seaweed, molasses and enzymes.
Blood Meal	12	0	0	Good nitrogen but expensive and has an unpleasant odor.
Bone Meal	0	10	0	Good photphorus and calcium source, raises pH.
Cattle Manure	2	1	1	Use composted only to avoid weeds, same for horse and other livestock manures.
Compost	1	1	1	Best all-around organic fertilizer.
Cottonseed Meal	7	2	2	Acid pH, trace elements, unpleasant odor.
Earthworm Castings	1	1	.5	Bacteria, trace elements, humus.
Fertilaid	4	2	0	Tankage, bacteria cultures, trace elements.
Fish Emulsion	5	2	2	Excellent foliar food, helps control insects. Fish meal is also good.
GreenSense	3	1	2	Composted manure, alfalfa, molasses, activated carbon, trace minerals.
Phosphate, Colloidal	0	16	0	Economic, long-lasting source of photphorus and calcium.
Poultry Manure	5	3	2	High in nitrogen, economically available, heavy metals.
Rabbit Manure	3	2	1	Not enough rabbits.
Seaweed (Kelp)	1	0	1	Trace minerals, hormones, root stimulators.
Sewer Sludge	6	4	0	More cities should produce and sell for lawn food. Avoid using on edible crops.
Sul-Po-Mag	0	0	22	Source of sulfur, potash and magnesium.
Sustane	5	2	4	Composted turkey manure.

moisture level rather than a wet, dry, wet, dry cycle. Newly planted trees should be thoroughly soaked every other week in the hot growing season and once per month in the cooler seasons. This watering should be done in addition to regular watering of the grass areas or planting areas surrounding the trees. Obviously, rain will alter this schedule. Once trees are established, a regular watering of the surrounding planting areas should be enough. During periods of extreme drought, the soaking procedure may need to be used again.

Pest Control

Spraying for insects and diseases on a preventative basis wastes money and adds unnecessarily to the chemicals in our environment. Sprays for insects and diseases should only be applied after pests are seen. Always choose environmentally safe alternatives. Aphids, for example, can be controlled with a strong blast of water and the release of ladybugs. Diacide is an excellent organic insecticide that combines D-Earth with natural Pyrethrum. Bacillus thuringiensis (Bt) is an environmentally safe control for cutworms, loopers and caterpillars. Ladybugs, green lacewings and trichogramma wasps provide excellent control of aphids, spider mites, worms and other small insects. Beneficial insects should be put out at dusk after wetting all the foliage in the garden.

Harsh chemical pesticides will probably continue to be used, but if just some of you gardeners elect to use some of the natural alternatives, we will have made a step in the right direction. Besides being extremely dangerous and harmful to people and pets, strong chemicals also kill the beneficial microorganisms, earthworms, insects, lizards, frogs, and birds in the garden.

Weed Control

Herbicide application under any tree is risky and should be avoided. Improvement of soil health, hand removal and mulch on all bare soil is all that is usually needed.

SHRUBS

Pruning

No pruning is required at the time of planting, and yearly pruning should be kept to a minimum, leaving the plants as soft and natural as possible. Pick-pruning of shrubs, although somewhat time-consuming, has always been my favorite method. Due to time constraints, a combination of light shearing and careful pick-pruning will create the best effect. Severe shearing or boxing should be avoided except in extremely formal gardens. Flowering shrubs, especially spring bloomers, need to be pruned immediately after flowering, not later in the season, so that no damage will be done to stems forming the buds for the next year's flower display.

Mulching

Shrubs should be mulched at the time of planting. The mulch does an excellent job of holding moisture in the soil, preventing weeds and keeping the ground cool, thus aiding in the quick establishment of root systems.

> ### USING MULCH TO PROTECT THE SOIL
> Because mulch slows down the rate of the rain entering the soil, it gives the soil a chance to absorb the water. Mulch also encourages microorganisms to work nearer the surface of the soil. Mulch also prevents weeds, maintains moisture, and keeps soil temperature cool.

Fertilizing

Shrubs should be fertilized the same as trees: fertilize in the early spring, again in early to mid-summer and a third time in the fall if the soil still needs improvement. As with trees, I recommend fertilizing the ground surface at the rate of 10 pounds per thousand square feet using a 100% organic fertilizer. Avoid a concentration of fertilizer at the trunk or main stem of the plant to avoid burn. A thorough watering should follow any application of fertilizer.

Watering

I recommend the same watering technique for shrubs as for trees. However, since the plants are smaller in size, they can dry out faster and a little more care is needed in monitoring the watering program. In the hotter parts of the state, which is most of the state, I recommend a sprinkler system unless you have an awful lot of free time to stand around at the end of a water hose. Above-ground bubblers and soaker hoses are quite effective and efficient, but I would avoid below-ground drip systems.

Pest Control

I recommend the same techniques for shrubs as explained previously for trees. Remember that effective pest control is greatly enhanced by keeping your plants as healthy as possible using 100% organic fertilizers and generous amounts of well-made compost. Insects and diseases primarily attack weak, unhealthy, stressed plants. Also remember that it's not necessary to kill every bad bug in your garden — a few are no problem and an important part of Nature's systems. A healthy population of beneficial insects is the best control.

Weed Control

Pull the weeds by hand and mulch heavily.

GROUND COVER AND VINES

Pruning

No pruning is required at planting time. The only regular ground cover pruning I recommend, other than edging as needed, is a one-time late winter or early spring mowing with a lawnmower set on its highest setting. Most ground covers used in large areas other than English ivy can be mowed, saving a lot of time and money. To prevent tearing the plants, sharpen the blades of the lawnmower and, if mowing large areas, stop occasionally to resharpen.

Vines should be kept trimmed back to the desired size and can be trimmed at any time. Prune flowering vines immediately after the plant has stopped blooming. Pruning at other times can eliminate the next year's flower production.

Mulching

Mulching bare areas should be done after the plants have been installed. Once the plants have established, mulching generally is not needed because the foliage takes over that function but remulching should be done if any bare areas appear during the season.

Fertilizing

The fertilization I recommend for ground cover and vines is the same as for shrubs. Remember that 100% organic fertilizers will give you the best results in the long run.

Watering

During the establishment period of ground cover, supplemental watering is usually needed in addition to the sprinkler system because the very small root systems of ground covers can dry out quickly. The key to the quick establishment of ground cover is keeping the soil evenly moist, not sopping wet. Mulch will help greatly in this regard.

Pest Control

Use the same organic techniques for ground cover and vines as mentioned previously for trees and shrubs.

ANNUALS, PERENNIALS AND HERBS

Pruning

Spent flowers and stems should be removed as they fade in order to encourage new blooms. Plants that have become damaged or diseased should be removed.

Mulching

Mulching the exposed soil around the plants should be done at planting and remulching should be done as any bare areas appear during the season.

Fertilizing

Annuals and perennials should be fertilized along with the trees, shrubs and lawns with 100% organic fertilizers. For additional flower production, use earthworm castings at 10 lb/1000 sq. ft. and bat guano at 10 lb/1000 sq. ft. in addition to the basic fertilization. Spray the plants at least twice per month with fish emulsion and seaweed. Epsom salts (Magnesium sulfate) at 1 tablespoon per gallon can be added to the spray solution.

Watering

Water as needed to maintain an even moisture level. Beds should never be soggy wet or bone dry between waterings. Occasional deep waterings are much better than frequent sprinkles. Potted plants should be watered daily through hot months and as needed during the cooler months. Once the plants have filled in solidly, use the same watering schedule as for the rest of the garden but check the pots often. Potted plants should be fertilized every 2 to 3 weeks with the following mixture. In a 20 gallon trash can add 1 cup vinegar, 1 cup Bioform, 1 cup Epsom salts, ¼ cup brewer's yeast, ¼ cup borax. Fill the rest of the can with water and use the mixture as a liquid fertilizer.

Pest Control

Use the same technique as explained earlier for trees. Special exceptions are covered at each specific plant in the pages that follow. The ground cover Pennyroyal Mint does a fair job of repelling fleas. Soap and water spray does an excellent job controlling aphids and Diatomaceous Earth and Diacide are effective in the control of many crawling insects. Bacillus thuringiensis controls cutworms, loopers and caterpillars well. Keeping the soil healthy and nutritious using generous amounts of compost will help keep pests to a minimum. Insects and diseases primarily prey on unhealthy or stressed plants. Don't forget to release ladybugs, praying mantids and green lacewings. Wasps, bees, dragonflies, fireflies and assassin bugs are also beneficial garden insects.

Certain plants do a good job of repelling insects. The best are Artemisia, Basil, Lavender, Pennyroyal Mint, Rosemary, Sage, Garlic, Santolina, Lemon Balm and Thyme.

Weed Control

I prefer hand pulling and mulch. Straight vinegar, 100 grain (10% acid) or stronger, is a good non-selection herbicide for hot weather weeds.

GRASS

Mowing

Maintenance of grass is the most time-consuming and expensive part of garden maintenance. Start by using the kind of grass that is most appropriate for your property. Mowing should be done on a regular basis and the clippings should be left on the lawn. No more than a third of the leaf blades should be removed in any one mowing. Mow grass according to the following:

- Bermudagrass, St. Augustine and Fescue — 3" height — once a week.
- Tifgrasses — ½" - ¾" height — two times a week.
- Zoysiagrass — 3" - 4" height — every other week.
- Buffalograss — 3" - 4" height — no more than once a month.

Scalping should never be done.

Fertilizing

Fertilization of grass can be handled in exactly the same manner as described above for trees and shrubs. In fact, the easiest and most cost-effective technique is to fertilize everything in your garden at the same time. Never use weed and feed fertilizers. They are very dangerous.

The "weed" part of the name refers to herbicides which kill plants. You should also avoid the often recommended high-nitrogen synthetic fertilizers. The overuse of inorganic fertilizers contaminates the soil and water systems with salt and cancer-causing nitrates. Organic fertilizers have lower levels of nitrogen and are naturally slow release. They have excellent buffering abilities and provide organic matter to build the humus in the soil.

> Top dressing lawns by spreading sand or loam is a mistake. Top dressing should only be done to level low spots and the best material to use is the same soil that exists in your lawn.

Watering

Again, watering is the most variable part of the puzzle, and I agree with most experts that water should only be used when necessary rather than on a calendar schedule. Occasional deep waterings are better than light sprinkles on a more regular basis. The amount of water to be used will vary tremendously from one site to the next depending on the soils, sun exposure, location in Texas, and how green you want your grass. Consistency is the key. Once your soil is organic and healthy, less irrigation will be needed.

Establish a level of moisture that you think is appropriate, one that isn't too wet or too dry, and stick with that program. Here's a general formula that I have used in the past that will give you a good starting point. It should be modified through the year for your

particular situation. If you have a sprinkler system, turn it on manually whenever water is needed.

Winter months — two waterings per month. **Spring and Fall** — water one time per week. **Summer months** — one watering every third to fifth day. **Newly planted material** — one watering every other day in summer, one watering per week in winter months. **Establishment period for grass** — water two to four times per day until established. **New Sod** — once a day until established — usually 7-10 days.

Obviously, rain, cloudy days, snow, wind, drainage, type of watering, amount of water per time and water bills all affect this schedule, but it will at least give you a starting point. It would be ideal to get to a point of watering no more than once per week.

WATER SAVING TIPS:

- Repair leaky faucets.
- Use a nozzle or spray gun on the hose so water can be shut off when not in use.
- Use a broom, not a hose, to clean paving surfaces.
- Collect rainfall in containers to use for landscape or pot plant watering.
- Put grass and planting beds on different sections of the sprinkler system when possible.
- Use above-ground bubblers instead of spray heads where practical.
- Run sprinkler system manually when needed rather than on a set schedule.
- Water during the cooler parts of the day to reduce evaporation.
- Avoid watering when windy, if possible.

Aerifying

Lack of oxygen is often the most limiting factor in the soil. Aeration is an important and often overlooked technique. To aerify grass areas, simply punch holes in the ground with any kind of equipment available in your area. Landscape contractors can be hired to do the work. It is amazing what this simple procedure can produce. Grass will green up as if fertilization has been done and the root systems of nearby shrubs and trees will appreciate the introduction of oxygen into the soil. Be sure to mark the location of the sprinkler heads to avoid damage.

Pest Control

Lawns rarely have insect problems if the soil is healthy and drains well.

Herbicides

Chemical weed killers are all very dangerous and I recommend staying away from them. They should only be used as a last resort, if at all. If you decide to use toxic herbicides, apply them with a wick applicator to avoid spray drift.

Vinegar (10% or 100 grain) sprayed on unwanted plants acts as an effective organic herbicide.

Over the past several years, an irresponsible amount of dangerous chemicals have been thrown, sprayed and poured on our gardens. I hope this maintenance section gives you some alternatives to help start reversing the cycle.

MAINTENANCE MISTAKES

There are many incorrect and unnecessary maintenance procedures. Some of the worst mistakes are as follows:

1. Spreading sand or loam on lawns in the spring.
2. Topping or dehorning trees.
3. Installing steel curbing at the edge of beds at sidewalks or other paving surfaces instead of properly lowering the grade of the edge of the bed.
4. Overtrimming trees and shrubs.
5. Using "weed and feed" fertilizer.
6. Misusing herbicides and chemicals in general.
7. Not removing sick or overgrown plants.
8. Over use of synthetic, high-nitrogen, salt-based fertilizers.

Here are three sources for information and products using the organic methods of fertilization and pest control.

Garden-Ville — 512-651-6115

B.I.R.C. — 415-524-2467

Howard Garrett Pay Telephone — 1-900-990-SOIL(7645)

ORGANIC PEST REMEDIES

DISEASES	CONTROL	APPLICATION
ANTHRACNOSE	• Liquid copper or Bordeaux	• Spray per label on new foliage in early spring.
BLACK SPOT	• Baking soda spray (4 TSP. PER GAL.)	• Spray lightly as needed.
BROWN PATCH	• Baking soda spray or Triple Action 20	• Spray lightly as needed.
FIREBLIGHT	• Triple Action 20	• Spray whenever problem arises.
GRAY LEAF SPOT	• Baking soda spray or Triple Action 20	• Light foliage spray as needed.
OAK WILT	• Maintain soil and plant health • Alamo	• Fertilize with organic techniques and water regularly. • Inject per instructions as a last resort.
POWDERY MILDEW	• Baking soda spray or Triple Action 20	• Light foliage spray as needed.
PEACH TREE CURL	• Baking soda spray • Garlic tea	• Spray in fall. • Spray in fall.
SOOTY MOLD	• Baking soda spray	• Light spray as needed.

NOTES:

(1) Using natural products and building healthy soil is the best treatment long term for all these problems. (2) Check local, state and federal restrictions. Which chemicals are legal and which are not is constantly changing. (3) Don't buy D-Earth from swimming pool suppliers; it is a completely different product. (4) An excellent all around spray for most insects and diseases is a mixture of garlic tea, BT and liquid seaweed.

WEEDS	CONTROL	APPLICATION
	• Vinegar 100 grain (10%) or stronger	• Spot spray full strength on sunny day. 20% food grade is even better. Strong vinegar is very corrosive.
	• Chop with a hoe or hand remove	• This is still legal!
	• Accept a few	• Many "weeds" are herbs, wildflowers and beneficial grasses.

NOTE:

Herbicides should be avoided. Good cultural practices, organic fertilizers, compost and soil activators will encourage good plants and grasses and discourage weeds.

Avoid soaps containing phosphates; use biodegradable kinds such as Shaklees Basic-H and Neo Life.

INSECTS	CONTROL	APPLICATION
APHIDS	• Water blast • Beneficial insects	• Use hose nozzle or a strong thumb. • Release ladybugs, braconid wasps and green lacewings.
FIRE ANTS	• *"Logic"* Fire Ant Control	• 1 lb/acre on dry soil when ants are foraging.
BAGWORMS **CATERPILLARS**	• *Bt (Bacillus thuringiensis)* • Beneficial insects	• Spray with 1 tsp. soap per gal. at dusk. • Encourage and protect native wasps. Release green lacewings and trichogramma wasps.
BEETLES	• Pyrethrum, Rotenone, Sabadilla	• Make sure beetle in question is harmful — many are beneficial.
BORERS, TREE	• Pyrethrum/rotenone	• Run stiff wire into borer holes. • Put insecticide into holes full strength and seal holes with putty.
CRICKETS **CHIGGERS** **CHINCHBUGS**	• Diatomaceous earth	• Dust infested area @ 1 cup/1000 s.f. • 2 tbsp. plus 1 tsp. soap per gal. Spray infested area.
CUTWORMS	• Diatomaceous earth • *Bt (Bacillus thuringiensis)*	• Pour a ring of material around each plant. • Apply per label at dusk. Add 1 tsp soap per gal.
ELM LEAF BEETLE	• *Bt (Bacillus thuringiensis* 'San Diego')	• Spray per label at dusk.
FLEA BEETLES	• Garlic tea/diatomaceous earth	• Spray at first sign of problem.
FLEAS	• Outdoors: *Diacide* or other D-E/Pyrethrum products	• 2 tbsp. plus 1 tsp. soap per gal. Spray infested area. • Bathe pets regularly in mild soapy water.
GRASSHOPPERS	• *Nolo Bait*	• Apply per label instructions.
GRUBWORMS	• Beneficial nematodes	• Per label instructions.
LACEBUGS	• Horticultural oil	• Per label instructions.
LEAFHOPPERS	• Praying mantids	• Release as necessary.
LEAFMINERS	• Don't worry about 'em	• Minor damage only, usually no need to treat.
LOOPERS	• *Bt (Bacillus thuringiensis)*	• Apply per label instructions at dusk.
MEALYBUGS	• Horticulture oil	• Label instructions.
MOSQUITOES	• *Bti (Bacillus thuringiensis* 'Israelensis')	• Put briquettes in standing water.
NEMATODES	• Beneficial nematodes	• Label instructions.
PECAN CASE	• Trichogramma wasp	• Release every two weeks during the spring. Start in mid-March or during first warm spell.
PILLBUGS	• Beer traps	• Cheap beer into a recessed container.
ROACHES	• Diatomaceous earth • Boric acid	• Dust infested area lightly. • Dust infested areas lightly (indoors only).
SCALE	• Dormant oil	• Label instructions in winter.
SLUGS **SNAILS**	• Beer trap • Diatomaceous earth	• Plastic jar or glass sunk into ground. • Dust infested area.
SPIDERMITES	• Beneficial insects • Garlic/pepper tea	• Release green lacewing and predatory mites. • Spray every 3 days for 9 days.
THRIPS	• Garlic/pepper tea	• Spray every 2 weeks or as needed.
WEBWORMS	• *Bt (Bacillus thuringiensis)*	• Spray with 1 tsp. soap per gal. at dusk.
WHITEFLIES	• Garlic/pepper tea • Yellow sticky traps	• ¼ cup/gal. Spray as needed. • Hang in infested area.

MAINTENANCE BY THE CALENDAR

January

Mow or hand remove grassy weeds, allow clover to grow. **Hand water** annual beds as needed. **Mulch** bare soil. **Prune** trees (major pruning). **Spray** dormant oil on Red Oak, Pecan, Crabapple, Euonymus, Holly, Camellia if serious infestations exist. **Fertilize** Pansies and other winter annuals with fish emulsion and seaweed. **Plant** shrubs and trees. **Prune** summer flowering shrubs. **Do not** prune spring flowering shrubs. Take mowers and power tools to repair shops now to avoid the spring rush. Don't forget to feed the birds.

February

Mow or spray winter weeds with vinegar. **Hand water** annuals. **Mulch** bare soil in all beds. **Prune** trees (major pruning). Prune roses back about 50% around February 22. **Fertilize** Pansies and other winter annuals with bat guano and earthworm castings. Fertilize all lawns, beds and trees with a 100% organic fertilizer **(first major fertilization)**. Add to the compost pile and feed the birds.

March

Do not scalp grass areas. **Hand water** annual beds as needed. **Mulch** all bare soil. **Mow or hand trim** ground cover beds. **Fertilize** all planting areas and grass with 100% organic fertilizer if not done in February. **Shift** or move any wrong color Azaleas while in bloom. Release ladybugs for control of aphids if necessary. Plant Petunias and other cool season annuals. Feed the birds!

April

Start regular mowing schedule and leave clippings on the ground. **Hand water** dry spots, annuals and newly planted areas. **Mulch** all bare areas. **Prune** flowering shrubs after they have stopped blooming. Release ladybugs for aphids on new growth. Watch for snails, pill bugs, cutworms, squash bugs, loopers and armyworms. Put roses on a regular care schedule. **Shift** or move any wrong color Azaleas while they are in bloom. Birds!

May

Mow regularly and leave clippings on the ground. **Hand water** dry spots, annuals and newly planted areas. **Mulch** all bare soil. Release ladybugs and green lacewings at the first sign of a problem. **Spray** all plants with fish emulsion and seaweed. Watch for mildew on Crape Myrtles, bagworms on conifers, whitefly on Gardenias and Ligustrum, aphids on new growth of everything. Watch for caterpillars on Boston Ivy. **Mechanically aerate** lawns. **Plant** warm season annuals. Turn the compost pile and feed the birds.

June

Mow regularly and do not catch clippings. **Hand water** dry spots, annuals, and newly planted areas. **Mulch** all bare soil. **Prune** away all dead or diseased wood. Release beneficial insects. **Fertilize** lawns and all planting areas with 100% organic fertilizer **(2nd major fertilization)**. Pinch buds of mums. **Mulch** roses. Watch for powdery mildew on Crape Myrtle, Roses and Photinia. Don't forget the compost pile and the birds.

July

Mow regularly and do not catch the clippings. **Hand water** dry spots, annuals, and newly planted areas. **Deep water** during the hot months. **Mulch** all bare areas. **Prune** all dead or diseased wood. **Fertilize** all lawns and planting beds with 100% organic fertilizer if not done in June. Watch for red spider mites on Marigolds, Junipers, and Verbena; they are usually at their peak during the hot, dry months. **Spray** all plants with fish emulsion and seaweed and feed the birds.

August

Mow regularly and leave the clippings on the lawn. **Mechanically aerate** lawns. **Hand water** dry spots, annuals, and newly planted areas. **Mulch** all bare soil. **Prune** all dead or diseased wood. Red spider mites are at their peak this month. **Spray** all plants with fish emulsion and seaweed. **Plant** Zinnias and Marigolds for fall color. Stop pinching Chrysanthemums the first of the month. Turn the compost pile and remember the birds.

September

Sow Bluebonnet seeds and other wildflowers. **Mow** as needed. **Hand water** newly planted areas and annuals. **Mulch** all bare soil. **Fertilize** all planting areas and lawn with 100% organic fertilizer. **Prune** all dead or diseased wood. **Spray** for insect or disease problems. Watch for fungus in St. Augustine lawns. Early September is last chance to **seed** or **hydromulch** Bermuda or ·buffalograss. Alternate choice is cool season grass (Fescue, Rye, Bluegrass), especially in a shady areas. **Fertilize** all potted plants with bat guano and earthworm castings. Fertilize all planting areas with 100% organic fertilizer if soil is not yet in healthy condition. Feed the birds.

October

Mow once per week at 3½". **Hand water** dry spots, newly planted areas and annuals. **Prune** all dead or diseased wood. Pull up spent annuals, cut off tops of spent perennials. **Divide** perennials. Force indoor bulbs. **Plant** shrubs and trees. Plant spring blooming perennials, cool season annuals, and wildflowers. Turn the compost pile and don't forget to feed the birds.

November

Mow regularly. **Hand water** dry spots. **Mulch** bare soil. Remove dead or diseased leaves and wood weekly by pick-pruning. Begin major tree **pruning**. **Plant** shrubs and trees. Plant Pansies and other cool season annuals. **Fertilize** Pansies or other winter annuals with bat guano and earthworm castings. Don't forget to feed the birds!

December

Put up the **Christmas decorations.** Do not **mow** unless winter weeds appear. **Hand water** annuals and new plants. Perform major tree **pruning** and remove mistletoe. **Spray** dormant oil on Red Oaks, Crabapples and Camellias, but only if heavy infestations exist. **Fertilize** Pansies and other winter annuals with fish emulsion and seaweed. **Plant** shrubs and trees. Don't forget to feed the birds.

TREES

EASY REFERENCE FOR TREES

EVERGREEN

Cedar
Cypress, Italian
Holly
Magnolia
Wax Myrtle
Live Oak
Palm
Pine

FLOWERING TREES

Cherry
Chitalpa
Crabapple
Crapemyrtle
Dogwood
Eve's Necklace
Goldenrain Tree
Hawthorn
Loblolly Bay
Magnolia
Peach
Pear
Plum
Redbud
Soapberry
Tulip Tree
Viburnum
Vitex
Desert Willow

YELLOW FALL COLOR

Ash
Buckeye, Mexican
Chitalpa
Crapemyrtle, White
Elm
Ginkgo
Goldenrain Tree
Maple, Caddo
Maple, Coral Bark
Oak, Bur
Pecan
Persimmon
Pistachio, Chinese
Redbud
Soapberry
Sweetgum
Tulip Tree
Walnut

ORANGE FALL COLOR

Ash, Texas
Plum, Mexican
Maple, Japanese

RED FALL COLOR

Crapemyrtle — Red, Pink, Purple
Cypress
Dogwood
Maple, Japanese
Oak, Red
Pear
Pistachio, Chinese
Sweetgum

WINTER BERRIES

Deciduous Yaupon Holly
Soapberry
Yaupon Holly

TREES

Ash, Prickly (*Zanthoxylum clavaheculus*) — Also called Hercules Club, is a small native tree with corky, spine tipped growths on the trunk and limbs.

Bay, Loblolly (*Gordonia lasianthus*) — White 5 petaled flowers with yellow centers in summer. Close kin of the Franklin Tree (Franklinia).

Buckeye, Texas (*Aesculus glabra arguta*) — Small native tree to 30', white flowers in spring. Foliage looks similar to Chestnut. Grows well in alkaline soils, sun or partial shade.

Buckeye, Scarlet (*Aesculus pavia*) — Small scale understory tree, beautiful chestnut-like foliage and red flower spikes in late spring. Needs plenty of light but shade in afternoon is best. Low maintenance plant.

Cedar, Incense (*Libdocedrus decurrens*) — Tall and straight, single dominant trunk, bark looks like redwood tree, foliage like arborvitae. Seems to do quite well here.

Cherry (*Prunus* spp.) — I have a wild cherry that blooms in spring with light pink blossoms, purplish summer color and beautiful scarlet fall color. That is all I know.

Filbert (*Corylus* spp.) — Small tree, twisted branches and twigs, foliage always looks slightly wilted. Distinctive plant for small courtyard or Oriental garden.

Jujube (*Ziziphus jujuba*) — Zigzag branches and stems. Small growing but quite interesting deciduous tree. Thornless cultivars exist.

Linden, Little Leaf (*Tilia cordata*) — Medium size shade tree with beautiful foliage and structure. There is a nice specimen in the Fort Worth Botanical Gardens.

Madrone, Texas (*Arbutus xalapensis*) — Evergreen tree to 30', beautiful smooth bark, white flowers in spring, red berries in fall. Hard to move. Native to Central Texas.

Magnolia, Bay (*Magnolia virginiana*) — Evergreen tree to 40', white flowers, leaves white beneath and beautiful when the wind blows them. Likes moist soil.

Oak, Lacey (*Quercus glancoides*) — Smallish oak with blue-green leaves. Native to Texas and has no problem with our soils. Deciduous, yellow fall color.

Oak, Vasey (*Quercus pungens vaseyana*) — Small growing, semi-evergreen. Drought tolerant and likes alkaline soil. Not readily available in the trade at present.

Oak, Monterrey (*Quercus polymorpha*) — Semi-evergreen tree from Mexico. Thick leathery leaves. May not be totally winter hardy.

Orange, Hearty (*Poncirus trifoliata*) — Small white flowers, oranges in fall, large stiff thorns, green branches in winter. Grafting stock for commercial oranges.

Palms — Windmill Palm (*Trachycarpus fortunei*) and Sabal Palm (*Sabal* spp.) are the two that do well here. Windmill is the most cold tolerant.

ASH, ARIZONA
Fraxinus velutina 'Arizona'
FRAK-suh-nus vel-u-TEA-na

Deciduous - Sun
Ht. 30' Spread 30'
DO NOT PLANT

HABIT: Fast growing junk tree. Brittle wood, yellow fall color, smooth bark.
CULTURE: Any soil, medium to heavy water and light fertilization.
USES: Fast growing temporary shade tree.
PROBLEMS: Borers, brittle wood, short lived, destructive roots.
NOTES: Do not plant! This plant was introduced as a drought tolerant, low maintenance tree but it is far from it. I once thought all Ash trees were bad because of this one. Native to Arizona and New Mexico.

ASH, MARSHALL SEEDLESS
Fraxinus pennsylvanica "Marshalli"
FRAK-suh-nus pen-cil-VAN-ik-a

Deciduous - Sun
Ht. 50' Spread 40'
Spacing 20'-30'

HABIT: Fast growing large compound leaves, dark green foliage, yellow fall color. Smooth, mottled bark when young, gets rougher with age.
CULTURE: Easy, any soil, medium water, light fertilization.
USES: Shade tree, fall color, background tree, mass tree planting.
PROBLEMS: Aphids in early summer.
NOTES: One of the best cultivars of Green Ash. Easily available in nurseries. Native to North America — cultivated.

ASH, RAYWOOD
Fraxinus oxycarpa 'Raywood'
FRAK-suh-nus oxy-ik-CAR-pa

Deciduous - Sun
Ht. 50' Spread 40'
Spacing 20'-30'

HABIT: Fast growing, upright, very dark green foliage, medium sized leaves with small leaflets, smooth greenish bark. Distinctive mahogany fall color.
CULTURE: Sun, any soil. Light to medium water and fertilization.
USES: Shade tree, good for courtyards or narrow areas.
PROBLEMS: Availability at this time is low but sure to improve.
NOTES: I was introduced to this wonderful plant at Black's Nursery in El Paso while working on *Landscape Design...Texas Style*. It is a real winner! Cultivated.

ASH, TEXAS (Native)
Fraxinus texensis
FRAK-suh-nus tex-EN-sis

Deciduous - Sun
Ht. 50' Spread 40'
Spacing 20'-30'

HABIT: Medium quick, large compound leaves with rounded leaflets especially on young growth, white splotches on trunk and limbs. Orange to purple fall color.
CULTURE: Easy, any soil, grows readily in alkaline soil, rock or steep slopes. Low water and fertilization needs. Needs excellent drainage. Easy to transplant.
USES: Shade tree, fall color.
PROBLEMS: Poor drainage, borers.
NOTES: One of Texas' best kept secrets. Closely kin to the White Ash *(F. americana)* — also a good tree. Should be used much more. Native to Texas. Excellent White Ash cultivars are 'Autumn Purple' and 'Rosehill.'

BOIS D'ARC (Native)
Maclura pomifera
ma-CLUE-ra puh-MIFF-er-ra

Deciduous - Sun
Ht. 40' Spread 40'
DO NOT PLANT

HABIT: Fast, spreading, dense foliage, thorny branches, "horse apples" on female trees, wood like iron. Yellow fall color.
CULTURE: Full sun, any soil, drought tolerant, low fertilization, good drainage.
USES: Shade, background.
PROBLEMS: Messy, hard to grow beneath, weak root system.
NOTES: Also called Osage Orange and Horse Apple Tree. Bois D' Arc trees should be removed to favor more desirable plants. Native from Texas to Arkansas.

BUCKEYE, MEXICAN (Native)
Ungnadia speciosa
oong-NOD-ee-uh spee-see-O-sa

Deciduous - Sun/Shade
Ht. 20' Spread 20'
Spacing 10'-20'

HABIT: Moderate growth, fragrant purple flowers in spring. Brilliant yellow fall color. Decorative 3-pod seeds on bare branches in winter.
CULTURE: Easy, any soil, little fertilization. Although drought tolerant can stand moist soils. Likes limestone alkaline soils, but will grow in any soil.
USES: Spring and fall color, understory tree, specimen courtyard tree.
PROBLEMS: Few if any.
NOTES: Can be easily grown from seed. The sweet seeds are poisonous to humans. Great tree — should be used more. Native to Texas and Mexico.

CATALPA (Native)
Catalpa bignonioides
kuh-TALL-puh big-none-ee-OID-ees

Deciduous - Sun
Ht. 60' Spread 40'
Spacing 30'-40'

HABIT: Large, fast, open branching, smoothish bark, very large light green leaves, white flower clusters in early summer, cigar-like seed pods.
CULTURE: Easy, any soil, rarely needs pruning. Grown in east Texas for the black caterpillars for fishing.
USES: Shade tree for large estates, parks, golf courses. Early summer flowers.
PROBLEMS: Messy flowers and catalpa worms in summer.
NOTES: Native to the southern USA.

CEDAR, DEODAR
Cedrus deodara
SEE-drus dee-o-DAR-a

Evergreen - Sun
Ht. 50' Spread 30'
Spacing 20'-40'

HABIT: Moderate, large conical shape, pointed top, foliage to the ground, foliage consists of small pine-like needles.
CULTURE: Any soil, good drainage, plenty of room.
USES: Parks, large estates, evergreen back drop.
PROBLEMS: Too large at the base for most residential gardens, freeze damage, diseases, bagworms and red spider.
NOTES: Sometimes called "California Christmas Tree." Graceful when healthy but I would not invest much money in this plant. Native to the Himalayas.

CEDAR, EASTERN RED (Native)

Juniperus virginiana
joo-NIP-er-us ver-gin-ee-A-nah

Evergreen - Sun
Ht. 40' Spread 20'
Spacing 20'-30'

HABIT: Single trunk, upright conical when young, spreading with age. Dark green juniper-like foliage, hard fragrant wood. Females have blue berries in fall. Mountain cedar *(Juniperus ashei)* is similar but usually has multiple stem trunk and does not suffer Cedar Apple Rust fungus.
CULTURE: Easy, any soil (even solid rock), drought tolerant.
USES: Shade tree, screen bad views, evergreen backdrop.
PROBLEMS: Bagworms, red spider mites.
NOTES: Is becoming more available as a nursery grown tree. Many are allergic to the pollen but it's in the air already from the wild trees. Native east USA and Texas.

CHITTAMWOOD (Native)

Bumilia lanuginosa
boo-ME-lee-ah lay-noo-gee-NO-sah

Deciduous - Sun
Ht. 60' Spread 30'
Spacing 20'-40'

HABIT: Slow, upright, dark stiff branches, small leaves similar to live oak. Yellow fall color, thorns. Resembles Live Oak at a distance.
CULTURE: Easy, any soil, sun.
USES: Shade tree.
PROBLEMS: Borers (bad problem).
NOTES: Not many have been used as landscape plants. I usually try to keep them alive if existing on a site. Native to south and southwest USA.

CHITALPA

Chilopsis x *Catalpa*
KY-lop-sis x kuh-TALL-puh

Deciduous - Sun
Ht. 30' Spread 30'
Spacing 20'-30'

HABIT: Cross between Catalpa and Desert Willow; lovely, open branching tree. Leaves are 6"-8" long and 1"-2" wide. Pink catalpa-like flowers bloom all summer.
CULTURE: Easy, any soil, rarely needs pruning.
USES: Distinctive garden tree; small area tree.
PROBLEMS: Few if any.
NOTES: This tree is relatively new to the scene and appears to be more healthy than either of its parent plants. This tree is a hybrid cultivar.

COTTONWOOD (Native)

Populus deltoides
POP-ewe-lus dell-TOY-dees

Deciduous - Sun
Ht. 100' Spread 50'
DO NOT PLANT

HABIT: Very fast, upright, light color bark, brittle wood, yellow fall color.
CULTURE: Very easy.
USES: Shade tree.
PROBLEMS: Short lived, destructive root systems, cotton from females, wind damage, borers, cotton root rot, very dangerous tree.
NOTES: Cotton from female plants is not only ugly but can do severe damage to air conditioners. This is one tree I almost always recommend removing. Native eastern USA to New Mexico.

CRABAPPLE

Malus spp.
MAY-lus

Deciduous - Sun/Part Shade
Ht. 25' Spread 25'
Spacing 15'-20'

HABIT: Spring flowers (white, red, pink), one half inch fruit matures in fall.

CULTURE: Easy, any soil, fall color is yellow usually, but red in some varieties.

USES: Ornamental tree, spring flowers.

PROBLEMS: Aphids, scale, red spider, web worms, rust, apple scab, fire blight, short life.

NOTES: At least 500 species exist. *M. floribunda* has white flowers with a pink tinge. 'Snowdrift' has white flowers, orange-red fruit. 'Sargent' has white flowers, dark red fruit. 'Callaway' has light pink flowers, large red fruit. 'Radiant' has single red flowers, red fruit. Native to China and Japan.

CRAPEMYRTLE

Lagerstroemia indica
lah-ger-STROH-me-ah IN-dik-kah

Deciduous - Sun
Ht. 25' Spread 15'
Spacing 15'-20'

HABIT: Slow, light smooth bark, small oval leaflets on compound leaves, flowers all summer (red, purple, pink, white). Fall color is red on all except white flowering varieties (yellow).

CULTURE: Easy, any soil. Add high phosphorus fertilizer to regular program to help flowers production.

USES: Ornamental tree, summer color, fall color, beautiful bare branches in winter.

PROBLEMS: Aphids, mildew, suckers at the ground.

NOTES: Do not trim back in winter — old wives' tale that it increases flower production — besides, the seed pods are decorative. Native to China.

CYPRESS, BALD (Native)

Taxodium distichum
tax-O-dee-um DIS-tick-um

Deciduous - Sun
Ht. 80' Spread 50'
Spacing 20'-40'

HABIT: Moderately fast, upright, pyramidal when young but spreading with age. Light green lacy foliage, reddish brown fall color. Branching structure is layered and distinctive. Root "knees" will appear in wet soil.

CULTURE: Easy, any soil except solid rock, drought tolerant, although can grow in wet areas. Cannot take any shade — must have full sun to avoid limb die back.

USES: Specimen, shade tree, background tree, fall color, delicate foliage texture.

PROBLEMS: Chlorosis occasionally, bagworms, crowngall occasionally.

NOTES: Likes well drained soils best. The often seen lake habitation results from a seed germination need and a protection against prairie fires through the years. Native east USA to Texas.

CYPRESS, ITALIAN

Cupressus sempervirens
coo-PRESS-us sem-per-VYE-rens

Evergreen - Sun
Ht. 40' Spread 12'
Spacing 6'-10'

HABIT: Slow, unusually upright, very dark green juniper-like foliage.

CULTURE: Relatively simple, any soil that is well drained.

USES: Background, tall border, screen, specimen tree for formal gardens, windbreak.

PROBLEMS: Red spider, bagworms, short lived in this area due to heat and humidity.

NOTES: Looks out of place in Texas unless you have formal Italian gardens, I would avoid this plant. Native to southern Europe.

CYPRESS, POND
Taxodium ascendens
tax-O-dee-um uh-SEND-enz

Deciduous - Sun
Ht. 70' Spread 30'
Spacing 20'-40'

HABIT: Rapid, more narrow than regular bald cypress, green earlier in spring and longer into fall. Leaflets spiral out from the stem and do not open. Long delicate filament-like leaves. Lovely, soft overall appearance. Rust fall color.

CULTURE: Easy, any soil, normal water and nutrient requirements. Can tolerate wet soil.

USES: Specimen, shade tree, mass planting, background tree.

PROBLEMS: Availability.

NOTES: Is not becoming more available. Also called *T. distichum* 'Nutans.' Best place to see this tree is the grove in Dallas at Central Exp. and McCommas. Native to southeast USA to Alabama.

DOGWOOD, FLOWERING
Cornus florida
KOR-nus FLOOR-eh-duh

Deciduous - Shade/Part Shade
Ht. 20' Spread 20'
Spacing 15'-20'

HABIT: Graceful, layered structure. Pink or white flowers in spring. Red fall color.

CULTURE: Needs loose, acid, well drained soil. Needs plenty of moisture but drainage is a must. Will do best in beds with heavy percentage organic material.

USES: Ornamental tree, spring flowers, red fall color. Oriental gardens.

PROBLEMS: Cotton root rot, soil alkalinity, borers.

NOTES: Would not be considered a low maintenance plant. This tree is native to acid, sandy soils like those in east Texas. Many improved cultivars available.

DOGWOOD,
ROUGH-LEAF (Native)
Cornus drummondii
KOR-nus druh-MUN-dee-eye

Deciduous - Sun/Shade
Ht. 15' Spread 15'
Spacing 6'-12'

HABIT: Small tree, blooms after leaves have formed in late spring with white flower clusters. White seed pods in late summer and purple fall color. Plant spreads easily by seeds and suckers but is not a problem. Stems are reddish and very decorative in winter.

CULTURE: Easy, any soil, drought tolerant. Very easy to grow.

USES: Background mass, understory tree, seeds for birds.

PROBLEMS: Few if any.

NOTES: Many have been cut down by people thinking they are weeds. This plant is graceful, tough and should be used more. Native east USA to Texas.

ELM, AMERICAN (Native)
Ulmus americana
ULL-mus uh-mer-ee-KAHN-uh

Deciduous - Sun
Ht. 70' Spread 70'
DO NOT PLANT

HABIT: Fast, gracefully spreading, large leaves, yellow fall color.

CULTURE: Easy, any soil, normal water and nutrients.

USES: Shade tree, large estate, park, yellow fall color.

PROBLEMS: Dutch elm disease, elm leaf beetle, cotton root rot.

NOTES: Ascending Elm is an upright growing version that was a failure. Neither of these plants are recommended, although I would certainly save any existing ones. Native to the eastern half of the USA. *Zelkova* is being used as an American Elm substitute. It is a similar tree but has more upright growth.

ELM, SIBERIAN

Ulmus pumila
ULL-mus PEWM-i-luh

Deciduous - Sun
Ht. 50' Spread 50'
DO NOT PLANT

HABIT:	Upright to spreading shade tree, leaves just smaller than American Elm.
CULTURE:	Grows anywhere.
USES:	Shade tree.
PROBLEMS:	Elm leaf beetle, Dutch Elm disease, brittle wood. Often confused with the excellent Lacebark (*U. parvifolia*).
NOTES:	Extremely unhealthy plant. Do not plant. I would even recommend removing existing ones. Native to Asia.

ELM, CEDAR (Native)

Ulmus crassifolia
ULL-mus krass-ee-FOLE-ee-uh

Deciduous - Sun
Ht. 80' Spread 60'
Spacing 20'-40'

HABIT:	Upright, moderate growth, yellow/gold fall color, irregular growth pattern, rough textured leaves.
CULTURE:	Any soil, drought tolerant but can stand fairly wet soil also.
USES:	Shade tree. Street tree.
PROBLEMS:	Aphids, elm leaf beetle, mildew, mistletoe.
NOTES:	Overused tree in North Texas. Referred to as "poor man's live oak." It is becoming more unhealthy every year. Winged elm (*Ulmus alata*) close kin, same characteristics with the addition of wings on the stems. Native south USA to west Texas.

ELM, LACEBARK

Ulmus parvifolia sempervirens
ULL-mus par-vi-FOAL-ee-uh sem-per-VYE-rens

Deciduous - Sun
Ht. 50' Spread 40'
Spacing 20'-30'

HABIT:	Upright and spreading, delicate foliage on limber stems, trunk bark is distinctively mottled. Fall color is so-so yellow.
CULTURE:	Extremely easy, any soil, drought tolerant although can tolerate wet soil. Incredibly healthy and easy to transplant.
USES:	Shade tree.
PROBLEMS:	None except very tender bark in early spring just at leaf break.
NOTES:	Often confused with Siberian Elm (*Ulmus Pumila*) which is a trash tree. Lacebark Elm is a perfect example of the introduced tree being better than its native counterpart. Sold as Drake Elm, Evergreen Elm or Chinese Elm. Native to China.

EVE'S NECKLACE (Native)

Sophora affinis
so-FORE-uh af-FIN-is

Deciduous - Sun/Shade
Ht. 30' Spread 20'
Spacing 10'-15'

HABIT:	Moderately fast, upright, usually in the wild as an understory tree. Pink wisteria-like flowers and black bead-like seed pods in fall. Bark, especially new young growth, is greenish.
CULTURE:	Easy, any soil, drought tolerant.
USES:	Small garden tree, specimen, natural settings.
PROBLEMS:	Few if any.
NOTES:	Also called Texas Sophora. Excellent small tree for residential gardens. Native to Texas, Arkansas, Oklahoma and Louisiana.

GINKGO
Ginkgo biloba
GINK-o bye-LOBE-ah

Deciduous - Sun
Ht. 50' Spread 30'
Spacing 20'-40'

HABIT: Unique, open branching tree with vibrant yellow fall color. Foliage is medium green, fan shaped and beautiful. Light color bark and slow growth.

CULTURE: Any well drained soil. Doesn't like solid rock. Moderate water and fertilization needs.

USES: Shade tree, fall color, distinctive foliage.

PROBLEMS: Female fruit stink, slow grower.

NOTES: Also called Maidenhair Tree. One of the oldest trees on earth and can be found on almost every continent in the world. Largest I've seen is in Frank Lloyd Wright's office garden in Chicago. First identified from fossil records in China.

GOLDENRAIN TREE
Koelreuteria paniculata
cole-roo-TEH-ree-ah pan-ik-you-LAA-tuh

Deciduous - Sun
Ht. 30' Spread 20'
Spacing 15'-20'

HABIT: Upright and open branching, yellow flowers in summer, decorative pods following.

CULTURE: Easy, any soil, moderately drought tolerant. Does not like heavy fertilization.

USES: Medium size shade tree, summer color. Good for hot spots.

PROBLEMS: Few if any, other than relatively short lived.

NOTES: Ugly duckling when small but develops into a beautiful tree. Native to the Orient. *K. bipinnata,* a close kin, is not as cold hearty.

HACKBERRY (Native)
Celtis occidentalis
SEL-tis ok-si-den-TALL-is

Deciduous - Sun
Ht. 50' Spread 40'
DO NOT PLANT

HABIT: Fast, short lived, will self propagate from seed every spring all over the place. *C. laevigata* is another less common variety.

CULTURE: Any soil, any condition.

USES: None.

PROBLEMS: Galls, borers, weak roots, brittle wood, short life.

NOTES: Do not plant any more and cut down the ones that sprout up! Native to North America. Chinese Hackberry (*C. sinensis*) is supposedly much better — longer leaves and no gall problem.

HAWTHORN, DOWNY (Native)
Crataegus mollis
kruh-TAHG-us MAH-lis

Deciduous - Sun/Shade
Ht. 25' Spread 25'
Spacing 10'-20'

HABIT: White flowers in spring, delicate foliage and red berries in fall. Flaky bark and usually multi-trunks.

CULTURE: Easy, any soil, drought tolerant.

USES: Understory tree, specimen garden tree.

PROBLEMS: Cedar apple rust, aphids and other insects.

NOTES: Found mostly in the higher, well drained rocky soils. Native to Texas and Oklahoma. Texas Hawthorn (*C. texana*) is quite similar.

Downy Hawthorn   *Downy Hawthorn*   *Texas Hawthorn*   *Reverchon Hawthorn*

HAWTHORN, WASHINGTON

Crataegus phaenopyrum
kruh-TEAGUE-us fa-no-PIE-rum

Deciduous · Sun/Part Shade
Ht. 25' Spread 15'
Spacing 10'-15'

HABIT: Upright, densely branching, thorns, red berries in winter, yellow fall color. Clusters of white flowers in spring, blooming later than most spring flowering trees.

CULTURE: Easy, not susceptible to rust.

USES: Specimen garden tree.

PROBLEMS: Some folks don't like the thorns — they don't bother me.

NOTES: Great introduced ornamental tree, more showy than the natives. Should be used more in this area. Native to east and northeast USA.

HOLLY, DECIDUOUS (Native)

Ilex decidua
EYE-lex dee-SID-you-uh

Deciduous · Sun/Shade
Ht. 20' Spread 15'
Spacing 12'-15'

HABIT: Bushy growth if not trimmed, small leaves, red berries on bare branches all winter long — on female plants only.

CULTURE: Easy, any soil, drought tolerant.

USES: Winter color, understory tree, specimen garden tree!

PROBLEMS: Suckers from base, buying male plants accidentally.

NOTES: Birds apparently do not like the taste of the berries. Judy and I had a deciduous Christmas tree one year using this plant. Best to purchase when the berries can be seen on the plant. The male is not worth much. Native to southeast USA to Texas.

HOLLY, YAUPON (Native)

Ilex vomitoria
EYE-lex vom-ee-TORE-ee-uh

Evergreen · Sun/Shade
Ht. 20' Spread 20'
Spacing 10'-15'

HABIT: Bushy unless trimmed into tree form. Light color bark, interesting branching. Red berries in winter on female plants.

CULTURE: Easy in all soils. Drought tolerant but grows much fastern when irrigated regularly. Can stand fairly wet soil.

USES: Ornamental understory or specimen tree. Good for courtyards and small garden spaces.

PROBLEMS: Occasionally leaf miners in summer — nothing serious.

NOTES: Native to central Texas — not north Texas.

TREES

HONEYLOCUST (Native)
Gleditsia triacanthos
glad-DIT-see-ah try-ah-CAN-thos

Deciduous
Ht. 50' Spr
Spacing 20'

HABIT:	Narrow, upright, open, lacy foliage, yellow fall plants have huge thorns on the limbs with trunk. Also has large dark brown beans in ......inter.
CULTURE:	Any soil, drought tolerant, tough.
USES:	Shade tree.
PROBLEMS:	Thorns, borers, die back.
NOTES:	If nice specimens exist on your property, try to use them, but I don't recommend planting new ones. Native east USA to Texas. The thornless hybrids do not seem healthy here.

LOCUST, BLACK (Native)
Robinia pseudo-acacia
row-BIN-ee-ah SUE-dough ah-KAY-see-ah

Deciduous · Sun
Ht. 40' Spread 40'
Spacing 20'-30'

HABIT:	Upright and spreading; small oval leaflets on large compound leaves; white flowers in spring, yellow fall color. Fast growing.
CULTURE:	Easy, any soil, drought tolerant.
USES:	Shade tree.
PROBLEMS:	Few if any.
NOTES:	Black locust is a beautiful tree that should be used in more small gardens and courtyards. Native to east and central USA.

MAGNOLIA
Magnolia grandiflora
mag-NOLE-ee-uh gran-dee-FLORE-uh

Evergreen · Sun
Ht. 60' Spread 30'
Spacing 30'-50'

HABIT:	Straight central stem, foliage to ground unless trimmed up. Fibrous, shallow root system. Large white flowers a few at a time in summer.
CULTURE:	Relatively easy although they like sandy acid soils best. Do not even try in solid rock areas. Will grow to 100' tree in deep sandy soils. Needs lots of room.
USES:	Specimen tree for large area.
PROBLEMS:	Chlorosis. Difficult to grow anything under this plant, continuous leaf drop.
NOTES:	Native southeast USA to east Texas. Saucer Magnolia (M. soulangiana) is deciduous pink flower in spring, grows 20'. Star Magnolia (M. stellata) has white flowers, is deciduous and grows to 12'. Both do better with some shade. Many cultivars exist. A wonderful dwarf variety is 'Little Gem'.

Magnolia soulangiana in spring.

Magnolia soulangiana in summer.

Magnolia stellata in spring.

25

MAPLE, CADDO
Acer saccharum 'Caddo'
A-ser sah-KAR-um

Deciduous - Sun
Ht. 60' Spread 30'
Spacing 15'-25'

HABIT: Upright to spreading, yellow to golden fall color.
CULTURE: Easy, any soil, drought tolerant. Grows well in rocky, alkaline soil.
USES: Shade tree, great fall color.
PROBLEMS: Few if any.
NOTES: Best large growing maple tree for this area. Has not been used enough. Red Maple *(A. rubrum)* has beautiful fall color but needs deep soil. Two good cultivars are 'October Glory' and 'Autumn Flame.' Trident Maple *(A. buergerianum)* is another good maple for alkaline soil.

MAPLE, JAPANESE
Acer palmatum
A-ser pal-MATE-um

Deciduous - Shade/Part Shade
Ht. 6'-20' Spread 10'-20'
Spacing 10'-15'

HABIT: Beautiful spreading branches on various sized varieties, some are tall growing, others dwarf; some red, others green. Over 400 varieties exist.
CULTURE: Easy, any soil, normal water and fertilization. Best in light shade.
USES: Specimen garden tree, understory tree, spring, summer, fall and winter color. Smaller varieties are good in pots.
PROBLEMS: Delicate foliage will sometimes burn in heat of summer, not harmful.
NOTES: Green variety is largest growing and toughest. 'Bloodgood' and 'Burgundy Flame' have red foliage color. 'Disectum' is the dwarf lacy leaf and 'Coral Bark' has bright red stems in winter. There are hundreds of choices, even variegated forms. Native to Japan.

Fall color 'Ribbon Leaf'

'Coral Bark' in winter

'Bloodgood' cultivar

Fern Leaf variety

Variegated cultivar

'Disectum' cultivar

MAPLE, SILVER

Acer Saccharinum
A-ser sah-kar-RINE-um

Deciduous - Sun
Ht. 40' Spread 30'
DO NOT PLANT

HABIT:	Fast growing, weak wooded, short lived junk tree.
CULTURE:	Grows about the same in any soil.
USES:	Fast growing temporary tree. Low quality firewood.
PROBLEMS:	Chlorosis, borers, cotton root rot, short life, weak wood.
NOTES:	Trash tree — do not plant! Native to eastern USA.

MESQUITE (Native)

Prosopis glandulosa
pruh-SO-pis glan-due-LOW-suh

Deciduous - Sun
Ht. 25' Spread 30'
Spacing 20'-40'

HABIT:	Interesting branching, spreading with age. Delicate foliage and subtle yellow flowers in spring.
CULTURE:	Easy, any soil, drought tolerant. Existing or newly planted mesquites can be killed by overwatering.
USES:	Shade tree for low water gardens.
PROBLEMS:	Borers, too much water.
NOTES:	Not as hard to transplant as once thought. Nursery grown plants are probably easier to keep alive. Native from Kansas to Mexico. Best collected trees are from the Corpus Christi area.

MIMOSA

Albizzia julibrissen
al-BIZZ-ee-ah jul-leh-BREEZE-in

Deciduous - Sun
Ht. 20' Spread 30'
DO NOT PLANT

HABIT:	Spreading limber branches that droop to the ground. Lacy foliage with small leaflets that close at night. Shallow, destruction root system.
CULTURE:	Needs lots of room and lots of water.
USES:	Not even good for firewood.
PROBLEMS:	Destructive roots, short lived, crowds out good plants.
NOTES:	Luckily it is dying out from disease. The ultimate junk tree. Native to India and Nepal.

MULBERRY

Morus alba
MORE-us AL-bah

Deciduous - Sun
Ht. 30' Spread 40'
DO NOT PLANT

HABIT:	Fast growing junk tree. Large varying shaped leaves. Very shallow and destructive root system. Smooth bark.
CULTURE:	Grows anywhere. Uses huge quantities of water.
USES:	None of redeeming value.
PROBLEMS:	Webworms, cotton root rot, destructive roots, ugly.
NOTES:	Undesirable tree. Do not plant! This is the most over-planted junk tree in the USA.

MYRTLE, WAX (Native)

Myrica cerifera
MY-ruh-kuh sir-RIFF-eh-ruh

Evergreen - Sun/Part Shade
Ht. 15' Spread 10'
Spacing 8'-12'

HABIT: Moderately fast, spreading, medium green, many small leaves, blue-grey berries in fall. Aromatic foliage dotted above and below.

CULTURE: Easy, any soil, drought tolerant.

USES: Specimen garden tree. Evergreen background. Good alternative to tree Yaupon.

PROBLEMS: Brittle wood, suckers.

NOTES: Birds like the berries. Dwarf Wax Myrtle *(M. pusilla)* also is available. Native to the southern states and the eastern half of USA.

OAK, BUR (Native)

Quercus macrocarpa
KWER-kus mack-row-CAR-puh

Deciduous - Sun
Ht. 80' Spread 80'
Spacing 20'-50'

HABIT: Spreading branching structure, large leaves, golf ball-size acorns, yellow fall color. Thick, cork-like stems, branches and trunk. Fast growing oak. Can grow to 150'.

CULTURE: Easy, any well drained soil including solid rock. Drought tolerant. Grows almost anywhere in the U.S.

USES: Handsome and hearty shade tree.

PROBLEMS: Few if any.

NOTES: Possibly my favorite shade tree. One of the longest lived oaks. Also called Mossy Oak or Cup Oak. Native to Texas, Oklahoma and eastern USA.

OAK, CHINKAPIN (Native)

Quercus muhlenbergil
KWER-kus mew-lin-BERG-ee-eye

Deciduous - Sun
Ht. 80' Spread 80'
Spacing 20'-50'

HABIT: Irregularly spreading, relatively fast growth, dark purple acorns, yellow-brown fall color.

CULTURE: Any soil, very sensitive to poor drainage, drought tolerant.

USES: Shade tree.

PROBLEMS: Wet feet and transplant difficulties.

NOTES: Easily confused with Chestnut Oak which will not grow here. Chestnut Oak has rounded lobes contrasted to the Chinkapin's sharp ponted edges. Native to Texas, Oklahoma and eastern USA.

OAK, DURRAND (Native)

Quercus durandii
KWER-kus doo-RAN-dee-eye

Deciduous - Sun
Ht. 60' Spread 40'
Spacing 20'-50'

HABIT: Upright, open branching, dense rounded top, smallish leaves with rounded lobes. Handsome tree. Reddish fall color.

CULTURE: Easy in any well drained soil. Drought tolerant and doesn't mind rocky soil.

USES: Shade tree.

PROBLEMS: Few if any. Not easily available in the nursery trade at this time.

NOTES: Bigaloe Oak *(Quercus durandii breviloba)* is a small growing close kin. Bigaloe is native to the north Texas area, Durrand is native Waco to central Texas.

OAK, LIVE (Native)
Quercus virginiana
KWER-kus ver-gin-ee-ANE-uh

Evergreen — Sun
Ht. 50' Spread 60'
Spacing 20'-60'

HABIT: Spreading evergreen shade tree. Small glossy leaves vary in shape and size. Single and multi-trunk. Black acorns.
CULTURE: Easy to establish, hard to maintain. Any soil. Drought tolerant. Needs thinning at transplant.
USES: Shade tree, evergreen background.
PROBLEMS: Aphids, ice damage, galls, oak decline. High maintenance tree requiring regular pruning, continuous leaf drop.
NOTES: Can freeze during severe winters. Looks its worst in spring when new leaves are kicking off the old leaves. Native to south, central and west Texas and southeast USA.

OAK, RED (Native)
Quercus shumardi or *texana*
KWER-kus shoe-MARD-ee-eye tex-ANE-uh

Deciduous - Sun
Ht. 80' Spread 80'
Space 20'-50'

HABIT: Graceful, upright and spreading, typically no central stem, fall color varies from brown to yellow to red. Fast growing oak.
CULTURE: Hard to establish, must have excellent drainage, any soil, drought tolerant.
USES: Shade tree, fall color.
PROBLEMS: Borers, scale, wet feet.
NOTES: Has always been one of my favorite trees but is the subject of a multimillion dollar tree problem. The problem with Red Oak is buying the right plant. Only two kinds will work in alkaline soils, Texas Red Oak *(Q. texana)* or Shumard Oak *(Q. shumardi).* Pin Oak *(Q palustris)* and cross breeds of Southern Red Oak *(Q. falcata)* and others are being sold in great quantities and will not survive here.

Pin Oak

Pin Oak foliage

Pin Oak branching structure

OAK, SAWTOOTH
Quercus accutissima
KWER-kus ak-cue-TISS-eh-mah

Deciduous - Sun
Ht. 50' Spread 40'
Spacing 20'-40'

HABIT: Fast growing oak, yellow-brown fall color. Golden-brown leaves stay on tree all winter. Long, narrow, serrated leaves.
CULTURE: Easy, any soil except solid rock. Doesn't like high pH soils.
USES: Shade tree.
PROBLEMS: Some chlorosis in highly alkaline areas. Wet feet.
NOTES: Excellent fast growing shade tree in deep soil areas. Native to the Orient.

29

OLIVE, RUSSIAN
Elaeagnus angustifolius
eel-ee-AG-nus an-gus-ti-FOAL-ee-us

Deciduous - Sun
Ht. 30' Spread 20'
Spacing 15'-20'

HABIT: Silvery-gray foliage, bushy unless trimmed. Relatively short lived.
CULTURE: Easy, any soil, drought tolerant, moderate fertilizer needs.
USES: Shade tree, gray color.
PROBLEMS: Too much water is the only serious problem.
NOTES: Likes the arid parts of the state more than here. Native to Europe and Asia.

PARASOL TREE
Firmiana simplex
fir-me-ANE-ah sim-plex

Deciduous - Sun
Ht. 70' Spread 50'
Spacing 20'-50'

HABIT: Fast, upright, smooth green bark when young, huge leaves, thick stems.
CULTURE: Easy, any soil, relatively drought tolerant, average water and fertilizer needs.
USES: Shade tree, conversation piece.
PROBLEMS: Coarse looking, weak wood.
NOTES: Native to China and Japan. Also called Chinese Varnish Tree.

PEACH, FLOWERING
Prunus persica
PROO-nus PURR-si-cah

Deciduous - Sun
Ht. 15' Spread 15'
Spacing 10'-15'

HABIT: Spreading ornamental tree, early spring flowers of all colors.
CULTURE: Easy, any soil, relatively drought tolerant.
USES: Ornamental spring flowering tree.
PROBLEMS: Borers, leaf rollers, crown gall.
NOTES: Flowers occur on second year's growth so prune carefully. Cultivated.

PEAR, BRADFORD
Pyrus calleryana 'Bradford'
PIE-rus cal-er-ee-AA-nah

Deciduous - Sun
Ht. 25' Spread 15'
Spacing 10'-20'

HABIT: Upright, very symmetrical, stiff, candelabra like branching. Early spring white flowers, red fall color. Short lived.
CULTURE: Easy, any soil, normal water and fertilization.
USES: Specimen ornamental tree, spring flower color.
PROBLEMS: Over used, short life.
NOTES: 'Aristocrat' is an excellent cultivar that has more open branching and long dropping leaves. It is much more graceful than Bradford. 'Capital' is a good narrow-growing cultivar. 'Whitehouse' has not had good reviews.

PEAR, CALLERY

Pyrus calleryana
PIE-rus cal-er-ee-AA-nah

Deciduous - Sun
Ht. 25' Spread 25'
Spacing 15'-20'

HABIT: More open than Bradford, limbs almost perpendicular to trunk. Red fall color.
CULTURE: Easy, any soil, average maintenance and water.
USES: Specimen ornamental tree.
PROBLEMS: Some think the thorns are a problem — I don't.
NOTES: This is the mother plant of the Bradford Pear. I like this plant better because it is more tree-like and graceful.

PERSIMMON, COMMON (Native)

Diospyros virginiana
dye-OS-pear-us ver-gin-ee-ANE-uh

Deciduous - Sun
Ht. 60' Spread 30'
Spacing 20'-40'

HABIT: Yellow fall color; dark, deeply fissured bark. Shiny foliage that gracefully droops. 1" orange fruit matures after first frost.
CULTURE: Easy, any soil, drought tolerant.
USES: Shade tree.
PROBLEMS: Webworms, messy fruit.
NOTES: This tree's few problems don't keep it from being an excellent shade tree. Japanese varieties are smaller plants but have large fruit the size of apples. Wooden golf clubs are made from persimmon. Native to Texas and the eastern USA.

PERSIMMON, TEXAS (Native)

Diospyros texana
dye-OS-pear-us tex-ANE-uh

Deciduous - Sun/Shade
Ht. 20' Spread 12'
Spacing 12'-15'

HABIT: Trunks and branches resemble Crapemyrtle. Small leaves, insignificant fall color. Slow growing. Small leathery leaves. 1" fruit turns black in fall.
CULTURE: Easy, any soil, drought tolerant. Can grow easily in rocky areas.
USES: Ornamental garden tree, decorative bark.
PROBLEMS: Few if any.
NOTES: Native to south and central Texas.

PECAN (Native)

Carya illinoinensis
CARE-ee-uh ill-e-noy-NEN-sis

Deciduous - Sun
Ht. 100' Spread 100'
Spacing 30'-50'

HABIT: Irregularly spreading, extremely graceful, yellow fall color, very long lived. Deeply rooted.
CULTURE: Easy, grows anywhere.
USES: Shade tree, pecan crop.
PROBLEMS: Worst is webworms which is mainly an aesthetic problem. Somewhat messy most of the time.
NOTES: Great choice for State Tree. The native varieties make better landscape trees than those bred for pecan crops. Native to North America.

PINE, AUSTRIAN

Evergreen - Sun
Ht. 30' Spread 30'
Spacing 15'-30'

Pinus nigra
PIE-nus NI-gra

HABIT:	Slow, thick, foliage to ground.
CULTURE:	Easy, any soil except solid rock.
USES:	Ornamental evergreen tree, background, evergreen screen.
PROBLEMS:	Chlorosis occasionally.
NOTES:	This tree and the Cross Pine (Japanese Black and Austrian Cross) are the best pines for this area. Red Cone Pine *(Pinus leucodermis 'heldreki')* is an excellent small growing pine. Grows to 15'. Native to Europe and Asia.

PINE, JAPANESE BLACK

Evergreen - Sun
Ht. 30' Spread 20'
Spacing 15'-20'

Pinus thunbergii
PIE-nus thun-BERG-ee-eye

HABIT:	Irregular form, foliage to ground. Central stem is not well defined.
CULTURE:	Any soil but solid rock but likes slightly acid soil best.
USES:	Evergreen ornamental, background, oriental gardens.
PROBLEMS:	Chlorosis.
NOTES:	Not quite as good as Austrian and Cross Pine. Native to Japan.

PINE, MONDELL

Evergreen - Sun
Ht. 40' Spread 20'
Spacing 12'-20'

Pinus eldarica
PIE-nus ell-DAR-eh-kah

HABIT:	Upright, medium green needles, foliage to the ground.
CULTURE:	Any soil, drought tolerant.
USES:	Shade tree.
PROBLEMS:	Pine tip moth.
NOTES:	Especially good in the alkaline clay soils. Also does very well in the drier parts of the state. Often sold as Eldarica Pine or Afgan Pine.

PISTACHIO, CHINESE

Deciduous - Sun
Ht. 70' Spread 50'
Spacing 20'-40'

Pistacia Chinensis
pis-TA-see-ah chi-NEN-sis

HABIT:	Fast, open structure; yellow, red and orange fall color — sometimes all colors on the tree at once. Light, smooth bark when young. Branching structure is poor when young but quickly fills out.
CULTURE:	Easy, any soil, drought tolerant.
USES:	Shade tree, fall color.
PROBLEMS:	Tip growth burns in early summer sometimes from too much water.
NOTES:	One of the best fast growing trees. Native to China. Texas Pistache *(Pistacia texana)* is native south of north Texas but has some freeze problems here.

PLUM, MEXICAN (Native)
Prunus mexicana
PROO-nus mex-ee-KANE-uh

Deciduous - Sun/Shade
Ht. 25' Spread 25'
Spacing 12'-20'

HABIT: Showy white flowers in spring and orange fall color. Exfoliating bark and graceful branching structure. Small edible plums. Has thorns.
CULTURE: Easy, any soil, drought tolerant.
USES: Specimen garden tree, understory tree, spring and fall color.
PROBLEMS: Insects chew on the leaves occasionally but no major problems.
NOTES: Wonderful tree, being used more and more. Smaller growing Hog Plum is less desirable. Native from Oklahoma to Mexico.

PLUM, PURPLE
Prunus cerasifera
PROO-nus ser-as-SIFF-eh-ruh

Deciduous - Sun/Shade
Ht. 20' Spread 15'
Spacing 12'-15'

HABIT: Small ornamental tree with bronze or purple foliage after pink spring flowers.
CULTURE: Any soil, moderate maintenance. Needs good drainage as most trees do.
USES: Ornamental garden tree, summer color.
PROBLEMS: Borers, possible freeze damage.
NOTES: 'Krauter Vesuvius' is most colorful and my favorite. Native to Asia.

POPLAR, LOMBARDY
Populus nigra italica
POP-pew-lus NI-gra eh-TAL-eh-kuh

Deciduous - Sun
Ht. 70' Spread 10'
DO NOT PLANT

HABIT: Slender and extremely fast growing junk tree. Very short lived.
CULTURE: Grows anywhere for a while.
USES: None.
PROBLEMS: Borers, root rot, short life, trunk canker, scale.
NOTES: Usually not healthy and never desirable — do not plant! Native to Europe and Asia.

REDWOOD, DAWN
Metasequoia glyptostroboides
met-ah-see-QUOI-ah glip-toe-stro-BOY-dis

Deciduous - Sun
Ht. 80' Spread 30'
Spacing 20'-40'

HABIT: Narrow and pyramidal, branches point up rather than perpendicular like Bald Cypress. Fine, lacy foliage, reddish-brown fall color.
CULTURE: Likes deep, slightly acid soils best but adapts to our alkaline soils quite well. Several large specimens are doing well in Dallas.
USES: Specimen garden tree, backdrop.
PROBLEMS: Chlorosis and foliage burn in shallow soils.
NOTES: An ancient tree native to China and Japan. Distinctive and worth trying.

REDBUD (Native)
Cercis canadensis
SER-sis kan-uh-DEN-sis

Deciduous - Sun/Shade
Ht. 30' Spread 30'
Spacing 15'-20'

HABIT: Wide spreading ornamental, purple or white spring color, yellow fall color.
CULTURE: Easy, any soil, drought tolerant.
USES: Ornamental garden tree, understory.
PROBLEMS: Borers, leaf rollers.
NOTES: White variety seems more healthy than the purple native. Crinkled leaf Mexican variety is the most drought tolerant, 'Oklahoma' has dark green glossy foliage and 'Forest Pansy' has red-purple foliage in summer.

'Oklahoma' Redbud

'Forest Pansy' Redbud

White Redbud

SOAPBERRY, WESTERN (Native)
Sapindus drummondi
sap-IN-dus druh-MUN-dee-eye

Deciduous - Sun/Part Shade
Ht. 40' Spread 30'
Spacing 20'-40'

HABIT: Foliage similar to Chinese Pistachio. White flower clusters in spring, golden fall color and winter berries, light gray bark and brittle wood.
CULTURE: Easy, anywhere, drought tolerant. Low fertilization requirements.
USES: Shade tree.
PROBLEMS: Few if any.
NOTES: Berries are used as a soap in Mexico. Also known as Indian Lilac. Native to west central and southwest USA.

SWEETGUM
Liquidambar styraciflua
lik-wid-AM-bur sty-rah-SIFF-flu-ah

Deciduous - Sun/Part Shade
Ht. 70' Spread 30'
Spacing 20'-30'

HABIT: Vertical, cone shaped, spreading with age. Red, salmon, orange and yellow fall color. Stiff branching. Round spiny seed pods.
CULTURE: Needs deep soil and prefers sandy acid condition — hates solid rock. Quite easy to transplant if given ample water.
USES: Shade tree, great fall color.
PROBLEMS: Chlorosis, dry, rocky soil.
NOTES: Native to East Texas and other sandy soil areas. Will grow much larger in sandy acid soils. Needs lots of water and acidifiers in alkaline soils. Improved cultivars include 'Palo Alto' and 'Burgundy' — excellent fall color.

SYCAMORE (Native)
Platanus occidentalis
PLAT-ta-nus ok-si-den-TALL-is

Deciduous · Sun
Ht. 90' Spread 70'
DO NOT PLANT

HABIT: Fast, large fuzzy leaves, white and gray flaky bark, yellow-brown fall color.
CULTURE: Anywhere, easy at first.
USES: Shade. The white trunks and limbs are lovely.
PROBLEMS: Messy, anthracnose, leafspot, aphids, scale, bagworms, borers, etc. Leaves are a nuisance. Destructive root system.
NOTES: Poor choice. The London Plane tree *(Platanus* x *acerifolia)* is supposed to be more healthy, but I still don't recommend it.

TALLOW, CHINESE
Sapium sebiferum
SAY-pee-um seb-eh-FARE-um

Deciduous · Sun
Ht. 30' Spread 30'
DO NOT PLANT

HABIT: Fast growing, short lived, poor quality shade tree. Yellow to red fall color and white berries in winter.
CULTURE: Easy, anywhere.
USES: Temporary tree.
PROBLEMS: Freeze damage, borers, cotton root rot, short life
NOTES: I used to mistakenly recommend this tree. There are lots of better choices. Native to China and Japan.

TULIP TREE
Liriodendron tulipifera
lir-ee-ah-DEN-dron too-li-PIF-err-ah

Deciduous · Sun
Ht. 70' Spread 40'
Spacing 30'-40'

HABIT: Straight trunk, smooth bark, leaves shaped like tulips, yellow fall color. Interesting flowers in late spring but sometimes hard to see.
CULTURE: Any deep, well drained soil. Does not like rock. High water requirement in heat of summer.
USES: Shade tree.
PROBLEMS: Leaf drop in mid to late summer.
NOTES: Also called Tulip Poplar, Yellow Poplar and Whitewood. Native to midwest, northeast and southeast USA.

VIBURNAM, RUSTY
BLACK HAW (Native)
Viburnum rufidulum
vi-BUR-num rue-FID-you-lum

Deciduous · Sun/Shade
Ht. 20' Spread 20'
Spacing 10'-20'

HABIT: Shrubby tree, glossy leaves, white flower clusters in spring, reddish fall color, blue-black berries late summer. Can grow to 40'.
CULTURE: Easy, any soil, extremely drought tolerant.
USES: Specimen garden tree, understory tree, background mass planting.
PROBLEMS: Few if any — practically maintenance free.
NOTES: Great shrub or little tree. Native to Texas and Oklahoma.

VITEX

Vitex agnus-castes
VI-teks AG-nus CAST-us

Deciduous · Sun
Ht. 20' Spread 25'
Spacing 15'-20'

HABIT: Called Lilac Chaste Tree also. Spreading, usually multi-stemmed, brittle wood, not long lived. Purple or white flowers in early summer. Nicely textured foliage.
CULTURE: Easy, any soil, drought tolerant.
USES: Summer flowers, foliage texture.
PROBLEMS: Short life, freeze damage.
NOTES: Native to Europe and Asia. Should not be used as a primary tree but rather as a secondary tree for special interest.

WALNUT, BLACK (Native)

Juglans nigra
JEW-gluns NI-gra

Deciduous · Sun
Ht. 50' Spread 50'
Spacing 20'-50'

HABIT: Open branching character, large distinctive leaves with evenly sized and arranged leaflets on each side of stem. Yellow fall color. Dark bark. Moderate to slow growth.
CULTURE: Likes deep soil, good drainage. Although tolerates alkaline soil, likes a more neutral soil.
USES: Shade tree.
PROBLEMS: Roots give off a toxin harmful to some other plants. Nut is almost all structure and no meat — not edible. Native to the southern USA.

WILLOW, DESERT (Native)

Chilopsis linearis
KY-lop-sis lin-ee-ERR-is

Deciduous · Sun
Ht. 30' Spread 25'
Spacing 15'-20'

HABIT: Open branching, delicate foliage, lavender, pink or white orchid-like blossoms in summer. No fall color to speak of.
CULTURE: Easy, any soil. Drought tolerant. Does better with more water.
USES: Specimen garden tree, summer color.
PROBLEMS: None.
NOTES: Lovely small tree, should be used more. Native to southwest USA.

WILLOW, WEEPING

Salix babylonica
SAY-lix bab-eh-LON-eh-kah

Deciduous · Sun
Ht. 40' Spread 30'
Spacing 20'-40'

HABIT: Graceful, fast growing. First tree with leaves in spring, last to lose them in fall — almost evergreen. Dense, fibrous root system.
CULTURE: Easy, any deep soil, high water needs.
USES: Softening effect, edges of lakes and streams, temporary tree.
PROBLEMS: Brittle wood, borers, cotton root rot, short life.
NOTES: Corkscrew Willows (*S. matsudana* 'Tortuosa') are more upright with twisted limbs and branches. Root problems are actually worse on other trees such as Mulberry and Sycamore. The native Black Willow (*S. nigra*) is not a very good landscape tree. White Weeping Willow (*S. alba*) has yellow stems and Blue Weeping Willow (*S. blanda*) is supposed to be a more healthy variety.

SHRUBS
AND "SORT OF" SHRUBS

EASY REFERENCE FOR SHRUBS

FOR SUN

Abelia
Barberry
Cotoneaster
Dwarf Crapemyrtle
Cleyera
Cyperus
Elaeagnus
Euonymus, Flameleaf
Forsythia
Hawthorn, Indian
Holly
Honeysuckle
Hypericum
Jasmine, Italian
Juniper
Ligustrum
Loquat
Nandina
Oleander
Photinia
Pomegranate
Smoketree
Spirea
Sumac
Viburnam
Yucca

FOR SHADE

Aralia
Aspidistra
Aucuba
Azalea
Camelia
Elaeagnus
Fern
Forsythia
Gardenia
Holly
Hosta
Hydrangea
Mahonia
Nandina
Podocarpus
Viburnum

SPRING FLOWERING

Agarita
Azalea
Camelia
Forsythia
Hawthorn, Indian
Jasmine, Italian
Ligustrum
Mahonia
Photinia
Pyracantha
Quince, Flowering
Rhododendron
Spirea

TREEFORM SHRUBS

Althea
Cleyera
Holly
Laurel, Cherry
Laurel, Texas Mountain
Ligustrum
Photinia
Viburnum

SUMMER FLOWERING

Abelia
Althea
Dwarf Crapemyrtle
Gardenia
Hydrangea
Hypericum
Jasmine, Italian
Oleander
Pampas Grass
Pomegranate
Smoketree
Texas Sage
Yucca

AZALEAS

KURMES

Adelaide Pope (deep rose)
Amoena (violet-red)
Bessie A. Dodd (coral pink)
Betsy (white)
Blaauw's Pink (salmon-rose)
Carror (rose-pink)
Christmas Cheer (red)
Coral Bells (coral)
Elaine (light pink)
Fedora (pink)
Flame (orange-red)
Glory (peach pink)
Hardy Firefly (orange-red)
Hershey Red (bright red)
Hino Crimson (red)
Hinodegiri (red)
Massasoit (dark red)
Mayo's Perfection (orange-red)
Mother's Day (red)
Orange Cup (orange-red)
Ruth May (pink)
Salmon Beauty (salmon)
Sherwood Red (orange-red)
Snow (white)
Tradition (pink)
Sweetbriar (white)

GLENN DALE

Amy (pink)
Buccaneer (orange-red)
Cascade (white)
Copperman (orange-red)
Driven Snow (white)
Fashion (red-orange)
Glacier (white
Green Mist (white)
Martha Hitchcock (white)
Treasure (white)
Trouper (red)

SATSUKI

Amaghasa (red)
Flame Creeper (orange-red)
Gumpo White (white)
Gumpo Pink (pink)
Okina-Nishiki (orange-red)
Pink Pearl (pearl-pink)
Wakaebisu (medium pink)

INDICAS

Fielder's White (white)
Formosa (magenta)
George L. Taber (white)
Judge Soloman (deep pink)
Pride of Mobile (deep pink)
Red Formosa (red)

GABLES

Herbert (lilac)
Lavender Beauty (lavender)
Rose Greeley (white)
Stewartstonian (red)

INDIAN HAWTHORN

Charisma (pink)
Dwarf White Entrantress (white)
Enchantress (rose-pink)
Indian Princess (pink turns to white)
Majestic Beauty (pearl-pink)
Spring Rapture (rose-red)
Springtime (deep pink)
Little Pinkie (rose-pink)
Clara (white) or Snow White
Ovata (white)

SHRUBS

Banana (*Musa* spp.) — Leafy tropical used as an annual or perennial if protected from the cold, 8'-12' tall. Plant in sunny spot with protection from the wind. Cut to the ground before a hard freeze and mulch over.

Bay (*Laurus nobilis*) — Bushlike herb, excellent landscape plant. Give southern exposure.

Bear's Breech (Acanthus mollis 'Latifolius') — Perennial with large oak-like leaves on thick stems. Dramatic flowers on long erect spikes. Grows in shade in well drained, fairly dry soil.

Cherry, Japanese Bush (*Prunus japonica*) — is well adapted and unique.

Butterfly Bush (*Buddleia*) — Tall, open perennial with lavender blooms in early summer.

Croton (*Codiaeum variegatum*) — Tropical shrub with colorful foliage of yellow, green and red. Use as an annual or move indoors in fall.

Elderberry (*Sambucus canadensis*) — White flowering native deciduous shrub or small tree. Shiny black purple berries. Thick succulent stems and red terminal branches.

Lilac, Persian (*Syringa persica*) — The only good lilac for this area.

Mock Orange (*Philadelphus coronarius*) — Fragrant, large growing deciduous shrub with dramatic white flower display in spring.

Rice Paper Plant (*Tetrapanax papyriferus*) — Perennial here, large dramatic leaves (2' in diameter) and creamy white flowers. Native to Formosa where it was used for making paper. Spreads.

Yesterday, Today and Tomorrow (*Brunfelsia latifolia*) — Shade loving tropical from South America. Blossoms open blue violet, fade to lavender and finally to white. The several variations in color appear on the plant at the same time — thus the name.

ABELIA
Abelia grandiflora
ah-BEE-li-ah gran-dee-FLORE-ah

Evergreen - Sun/Part Shade
Ht. 6'-8' Spread 6'-8'
Spacing 3'-6'

HABIT: Summer flowering shrub, tiny white or pink flowers. New growth in long shoots, bronze foliage color.
CULTURE: Easy, any soil, drought tolerant.
USES: Boundary hedge, screen, barrier. Dwarf varieties are good for mass plantings.
PROBLEMS: Few, plant looks bad when sheared into hedge.
NOTES: Dwarf varieties (3'-5' ht.), are available which are suited to smaller gardens: 'Sherwood,' 'Prostrata' and 'Edward Goucher.' Abelia is native to Asia.

AGARITA (Native)
Berberis trifoliolata
BER-ber-is try-fole-ee-o-LAY-tuh

Evergreen - Sun/Shade
Ht. 3'-6' Spread 3'-6'
Spacing 3'

HABIT: Spiny leaves always in threes. Yellow flowers in spring. Red berries in May. Irregular branching pattern which is more open in shade, tighter in full sun.
CULTURE: Easy, any well drained soil, drought tolerant.
USES: Evergreen border, boundary or background plant.
PROBLEMS: None.
NOTES: Native central and west Texas to Mexico. Also called Desert Holly.

ALTHEA
Hibiscus syriacus
Hi-BIS-kus si-ri-AH-kus

Deciduous - Sun/Shade
Ht. 10'-15' Spread 8'-10'
Spacing 8'-10'

HABIT: Summer flowering shrub, upright growth. Bare branches in winter. Yellow fall color.
CULTURE: Easy, any soil, fairly drought tolerant.
USES: Summer flowers.
PROBLEMS: Cotton root rot, aphids.
NOTES: Also called Rose of Sharon; should always be used with evergreens since it is so homely in the winter. Native to Asia.

AMERICAN BEAUTYBERRY (Native)
Callicarpa americana
cal-eh-CAR-pah a-mer-ee-KAHN-uh

Deciduous - Sun/Shade
Ht. 4'-8' Spread 5'-8'
Spacing 3'-5'

HABIT: Sprawling native shrub with insignificant pink flowers in spring and extremely showy purple berries in fall which last into the winter.
CULTURE: Well drained soil is important but adapts to any soil type. Very easy to grow.
USES: Free-form shrub or mass planting. Fall berry color.
PROBLEMS: Few if any.
NOTES: Versatile, carefree plant. Does not work well for cutting — berries fall off. White berried plants are available. Native eastern USA to Texas.

ARALIA

Fatsia japonica
FAT-si-ah jah-PON-eh-kah

Evergreen - Shade
Ht. 4'-6' Spread 4'-6'
Spacing 3'-4'

HABIT: Single stem, large tropical-looking leaves, rounded overall shape.
CULTURE: Needs well prepared bed, good drainage and protection from freezing weather.
USES: Shade gardens, Oriental gardens, tropical effects, coarse texture.
PROBLEMS: Aphids on new growth and freeze damage.
NOTES: Severe winter can kill this plant. Native to Japan.

ARBORVITAE

Thuja occidentalis
thu-ya ok-si-den-TALL-is

Evergreen - Sun
Ht. 25' Spread 15'
DO NOT PLANT

HABIT: Upright, multi-trunked evergreen shrub or small tree. Plated or juniper-like foliage.
Tight, pear-like shape when young, opening with age.
CULTURE: Grows anywhere.
USES: Cemeteries are the primary habitat of this plant.
PROBLEMS: Every insect known to man either eats or lives in this plant.
NOTES: The photo makes the plant look decent — it is not! Native to Northeast USA.

ASPIDISTRA

Aspidistra eliator
as-pi-DIS-tra ee-LAY-she-or

Evergreen - Shade
Ht. 24" Spread 24"
Spacing 18"

HABIT: Dark-green, large-leafed foliage plant. Leaves sprout from the ground. Spreads by rhizomes.
CULTURE: Easy, any well drained soil. Shade and plenty of water.
USES: Tall ground cover, coarse texture, low light area. Container plant.
PROBLEMS: Edges of foliage get ragged, especially in windy areas. Grasshoppers occasionally.
NOTES: Called Cast Iron Plant and Barroom Plant because of its toughness. Native to Japan.

AUCUBA

Aucuba japonica
ah-CUBE-ah jah-PON-eh-kah

Evergreen - Shade
Ht. 5'-6' Spread 5'-6'
Spacing 3'

HABIT: Upright on thick green stems. Yellow spots on long oval leaves.
CULTURE: Shade, moist soil and good drainage.
USES: Background, coarse texture, screen or accent plant.
PROBLEMS: Scale, nematodes, mealy bugs, spider mites — although none of these are serious.
NOTES: Also available in green and dwarf forms. Judy still does not like the spotty ones. I do.
Native to Japan.

AZALEA
Rhododendron spp.
row-doe-DEN-dron

Evergreen · Shade/Part Shade
Ht. 3'-6' Spread 3'-6'
Spacing 3'-6'

HABIT: Fibrous rooted shrubs with spectacular spring colors of red, white, pink, lavender and all sorts of combinations. Some varieties have attractive evergreen foliage, others are deciduous.

CULTURE: Must be grown in special beds of mostly organic material — 1/2 shredded pine bark or cotton gin trash and 1/2 peat moss is a good mixture.

USES: Evergreen hedge or mass, spring color.

PROBLEMS: Summer heat, chlorosis, poor drainage, scale and spider mites.

NOTES: Indica Azaleas such as 'Fielder's White' and 'Pride of Mobile' can take more sun and are more open growing. Kurume Azaleas such as 'Hino Crimson,' 'Snow,' 'Coral Bells' are tighter growing and need more shade. Gumpos are dwarf and bloom later than all other Azaleas. Huge numbers of species, varieties and cultivars are native to various parts of the world.

BAMBOO
Bambusa spp.
bam-BEW-sa

Evergreen · Sun/Part Shade
Ht. 2'-30' Spread Unlimited
Spacing 2'-4'

HABIT: Giant varieties and low growing ground covers, all bamboos spread like grasses. New sprouts come up once per year in the spring.

CULTURE: Best in partial shade, any soil, no special needs.

USES: Evergreen background, container plant.

PROBLEMS: Spreads and invades other plants. Some varieties will freeze in winter.

NOTES: Spreading can be controlled by kicking over the shoots just as they emerge in the spring. The last version of *Plants of the Metroplex* had black bamboo on the cover. It was an idiotic cover but the plant is quite interesting. Native to Asia.

BARBERRY, RED
Berberis thunbergii atropurpurea
BER-ber-is thun-BERG-ee-eye at-trow-pur-pew-RI-ah

Semi-Deciduous · Sun/Shade
Ht. 3'-6' Spread 3'-6'
Spacing 2'-3'

HABIT: Thorny, dense, yellow flowers in spring, red foliage in summer. Regular and dwarf forms are available. Mentor has green foliage in summer with red fall and winter color.

CULTURE: Easy, any soil, drought tolerant.

USES: Colorful barrier or hedge.

PROBLEMS: None serious.

NOTES: Thorns create a good barrier. The dwarf pygmy variety is an ugly little thing at first. Mentor barberry *(Berberis x mentorensis)* is larger growing green plant with red fall and winter color. 'Rose Glow' is a pink tinged cultivar. Can withstand drought and very low temperatures. Native to Japan.

BOXWOOD
Buxus spp.
BUX-us

Evergreen · Sun/Part Shade
Ht. 3'-5' Spread 3'
Spacing 2'-3'

HABIT: Compact shrub with rounded leaves. Medium to light green color and soft texture. Shallow roots.

CULTURE: Any well drained soil, moderate water and fertilizer needs.

USES: Border, low hedge, foundation planting.

PROBLEMS: Nematodes, leaf miners, scale, soil fungus and freeze damages.

NOTES: Not recommended unless a short clipped hedge is needed. Can be kept trimmed to 12" height. Native to Japan, Asia, Europe and North Africa. *B. koreana* 'Green Mountain' is a great looking compact form.

BIRD OF PARADISE (Native)

Caesalpinia gilliesii
Sez-al-PEN-ee-ah gill-EE-see-eye

Deciduous · Sun
Ht. 8'-15' Spread 10'-15'
Spacing 8'-10'

HABIT:	Small decorative tree or large shrub, dramatic yellow flowers spring and summer. Finely textured foliage.
CULTURE:	Easy, any soil, drought tolerant.
USES:	Ornamental tree, yellow summer flowers.
PROBLEMS:	Few if any.
NOTES:	Native central USA to Texas, Argentina and Uruguay. I have heard tales of 20' specimens along the Red River.

BUCKTHORN, CAROLINA (Native)

Rhamnus caroliniana
RAM-nus care-o-lin-ee-ANE-uh

Deciduous · Sun/Shade
Ht. 15' Spread 15'
Spacing 4'-10'

HABIT:	Bushy shrub or small tree. Large glossy leaves, yellow-orange fall color, red berries in late summer turning black in fall. Can grow to 30'.
CULTURE:	Easy in any soil with good drainage. Drought tolerant.
USES:	Specimen understory plant, ornamental tree, background plant.
PROBLEMS:	Few if any.
NOTES:	Also called Indian Cherry, this is a beautiful plant that should certainly be used more.

CAMELIA

Camelia spp.
cam-ME-li-ah

Evergreen · Part Shade
Ht. 6'-8' Spread 3'-6'
Spacing 3'-5'

HABIT:	Dark glossy foliage with flowers from fall to early spring. Slow growing.
CULTURE:	Needs loose well drained acid soil and protection from winter winds for best performance. Filtered light is best sun exposure. Full sun in the afternoon will burn foliage. Fertilize with special camelia food starting just after blooms fade in spring. Osmacote is good and so is a mixture of fish emulsion, cottonseed meal, and copperas.
USES:	Evergreen accent plant, border, container plant.
PROBLEMS:	Scale, aphids, winter damage, iron deficiency.
NOTES:	Native to China and Japan. Over 5,000 varieties. *Camelia sasanqua* 'White Dove' is a good choice. *Camelia japonica* has larger leaves and flowers. Sasanquas are easier to grow than Japonicas. Japonicas have the most showy blooms. The Dallas Camelia Society puts out an excellent pamphlet on growing camelias in the DFW area.

CLEYERA

Ternstromia gymnanthera
tern-STROH-me-ah gym-NAN-tha-rah

Evergreen · Sun/Part Shade
Ht. 4'-10' Spread 4'-6'
Spacing 3'

HABIT:	Soft, glossy foliage, reddish color especially in the spring and fall. Insignificant flowers. Berries ripen in late summer.
CULTURE:	Good drainage critical to avoid root rot. Do not box or shear this plant.
USES:	Background, border or accent plant. Can be trimmed into small ornamental tree and does well in containers.
PROBLEMS:	Aphids on new growth, root rot in wet soil. Healthy if planted properly.
NOTES:	Native to the Orient. Sometimes incorrectly sold as *Cleyera japonica*.

CORALBERRY (Native)
Symphoricarpos orbiculatus
sim-for-eh-CAR-pus or-bic-cue-LAY-tus

Deciduous - Sun/Shade
Ht. 2'-3' Spread 5'
Spacing 2'-3'

HABIT: Blue-green foliage, low growing, spreads by root suckers to form a shrubby thicket. Small pink or white flowers in spring. Berries form in summer along the stem and remain with their red-purple color after the leaves drop in fall. Can grow as tall as 6'.
CULTURE: Easy, any soil, drought tolerant. Cut to the ground in late winter.
USES: Naturalizing shrub, winter berry color. Tall ground cover.
PROBLEMS: Mildew sometimes.
NOTES: Too many people mow the plant down. If it exists on a site, try to save it. Also called Indian-Currant Snowberry. Native eastern USA to Texas and Mexico.

COTONEASTER, GRAY
Cotoneaster glaucophylla
co-ton-ee-AS-ter glau-co-FILE-ah

Evergreen - Sun
Ht. 2'-3' Spread 3'-4'
Spacing 2'-3'

HABIT: Low, very compact and dense, small gray leaves.
CULTURE: Any soil with excellent drainage. Can stand extreme heat and reflected light. Needs to be in full sun.
USES: Low mass, color contrast.
PROBLEMS: Fireblight, too much water.
NOTES: Not as healthy as *Cotoneaster horizontalis*. Native to China.

COTONEASTER, ROCK
Cotoneaster horizontalis
co-ton-ee-AS-ter hor-eh-zon-TALL-is

Deciduous - Sun
Ht. 2'-3' Spread 5'-6'
Spacing 2'-3'

HABIT: Low, horizontal, spreading, branches are layered and arch downward. Very graceful. Reddish-purple fall color and bare branches in winter. Small pink flowers in late spring.
CULTURE: Must have good drainage. Well prepared beds are best and it likes being on the dry side.
USES: Mass planting, accent, distinctive texture.
PROBLEMS: Several insects and fireblight can attack this plant if in stress.
NOTES: *C. dameri* is similar to Rock Cotoneaster but smaller and has larger flowers in the spring. Native to China.

CRAPEMYRTLE, DWARF
Lagerstroemia indica
lah-ger-STROH-me-ah IN-dik-ah

Deciduous - Sun
Ht. 5'-8' Spread 6'-8'
Spacing 3'-8'

HABIT: Small version of the crapemyrtle tree. Blooms all summer in colors of red, pink, white and lavender. White variety has yellow fall color. Others have red.
CULTURE: Easy, any soil in full sun. **Do not** prune back — let it grow! Can be pick-pruned lightly to maintain miniature size.
USES: Specimen, summer color, container plant.
PROBLEMS: Aphids on new growth, powdery mildew.
NOTES: Photo shows the best I've seen — it belongs to Laura Cates. Fantastic plant! Native to China.

CYPERUS

Cyperus alternifolius
cy-PEAR-us all-ter-ni-FOAL-ee-us

Perennial · Sun/Part Shade
Ht. 4'-8' Spread 4'-8'
Spacing 2'-3'

HABIT: Light and graceful plant with thin upright shoots. Dies to ground each winter but returns in the spring. Plant early in the season so root system will develop fully before freeze. More like a shrub than a flower.

CULTURE: Likes good planting soil best. Grows well in wet areas and even under water.

USES: Accent plant, distinctive foliage, bog or aquatic plant.

PROBLEMS: Grasshoppers, severe winter might kill the plant. No problem — buy another one. It is worth it.

NOTES: Fun for kids to cut stems in late winter. Remove foliage and put in water upside down — will sprout and root for planting outside the following spring. Also called Umbrella Plant. Native to Madagascar.

ELAEAGNUS

Elaeagnus macrophylla
eel-ee-AG-nus mac-crow-FILE-ah

Evergreen · Sun/Part Shade
Ht. 6'-8' Spread 6'-8'
Spacing 3'-4'

HABIT: Tough, gray-green plant. New growth in long shoots that arch out and down. Fragrant fall blooms hidden within the foliage. Fruit in spring is tasty and good for jellies.

CULTURE: Any soil, anywhere, fairly drought tolerant. Responds well to shearing if necessary.

USES: Border, background, screen.

PROBLEMS: None other than its pruning requirements.

NOTES: 'Ebbenji' is my favorite since it seems to be the most compact form. *E. pungens* is the larger growing and less desirable variety and has hidden thorns. Also called Silverberry. Native to Japan, Europe, Asia and North America.

EUONYMUS

Euonymus japonicus
ewe-ON-eh-mus jah-PON-eh-kus

Evergreen · Sun/Shade
Ht. 5'-8' Spread 4'-6'
DO NOT PLANT

HABIT: Upright thick stems, thick waxy leaves. Also called Evergreen Euonymus.

CULTURE: Any soil, anywhere.

USES: None — do not plant!

PROBLEMS: You name it! Scale, powdery mildew, aphids, leaf spots, crown gall, anthracnose, nematodes, heat ... etc.

NOTES: This plant is for people that wear leisure suits. Probably the worst plant you can buy. The yellow variegated varieties are disgusting even when healthy which is not often. Native to Japan.

EUONYMUS, FLAMELEAF

Euonymus alatus
ewe-ON-eh-mus al-LAY-tus

Deciduous · Sun/Part Shade
Ht. 8'-15' Spread 8'-15'
Spacing 4'-8'

HABIT: Thick, winged stems. Excellent red fall color.

CULTURE: Any soil, sun or shade. Best fall color in sun. Moderate water and fertilization requirements.

USES: Specimen, accent, fall color. Can be trimmed into small tree.

PROBLEMS: None serious.

NOTES: Called Burning Bush. Native to northeast Asia and China. 'Compacta' is the dwarf version and better for small gardens. 'Rudy Haag' is even smaller growing — 4'-5' height. They can be planted 3'-4' apart.

FERN, HOLLY

Cyrtomium falcatum
sir-TOE-me-um foul-KA-tum

Evergreen - Shade/Part Shade
Ht. 2' Spread 2'-3'
Spacing 1'-2'

HABIT: Low growing, compact, evergreen clumps. Dark green fronds.
CULTURE: Likes moist, well drained, highly organic soil in partial or full shade.
USES: Mass planting, softening element and good in containers.
PROBLEMS: Sunburn and freeze damage are the only dangers. Caterpillars occasionally.
NOTES: Also called Japanese Holly Fern. The dark spots under the leaves (fronds) are spores — not insects, so do not spray them. Native to Asia, South Africa and Polynesia.

FERN, WOOD

Dryopteris spp.
dry-OP-ter-is

Perennial - Sun/Part Shade
Ht. 18"-24" Spread 2'-3'
Spacing 12"-18"

HABIT: Low spreading fern. Delicate, deeply cut fronds, light green color giving good contrast with darker plants.
CULTURE: Needs shade or filtered light. Can grow in any soil but likes loose well drained beds best.
USES: Great for a softening effect in almost any garden.
PROBLEMS: None.
NOTES: Fern is in this section because it is more like a low shrub than a flower. Mysterious dark spots under leaves are spores, not insects. Plant from 4" pots. Native to everywhere.

FORSYTHIA

Forsythia intermedia
for-SITH-ee-ah in-ter-ME-dee-ah

Deciduous - Sun/Part Shade
Ht. 6'-7' Spread 5'-6'
Spacing 3'-4'

HABIT: Fountain-like growth, bare branches covered with bright yellow bell shaped flowers in early spring. Flowers last about 2 weeks.
CULTURE: Any soil, sun or shade. Better flower production in full sun. Good drainage is important. Prune after blooms fade.
USES: Specimen, background plant, yellow spring color and cut flowers.
PROBLEMS: None that are too serious.
NOTES: Best to use with evergreen plants since winter look is bare and uninteresting. Forsythia should at least be planted in the utility area or cutting garden just for the flowers. Native to China. 'Linwood Gold' and 'Spectabilis' are two excellent choices of the many available cultivars.

FOUNTAIN GRASS

Pennisetum spp.
pen-eh-SEE-tum

Perennial - Sun
Ht. 3'-4' Spread 3'-4'
Spacing 3'-4'

HABIT: Showy ornamental grass, slender leaves and flower plumes from July to October.
CULTURE: Easy to grow in most any soil in sun to light shade. Moderate water and fertilizer requirements.
USES: Specimen, medium height border, summer flowers.
PROBLEMS: None.
NOTES: Several similar varieties available with different heights and flower colors. Native to Central America.

GARDENIA

Gardenia jasminoides
gar-DEN-ee-ah jas-mi-NOID-ease

Evergreen · Shade/Part Shade
Ht. 4'-6' Spread 3'-5'
Spacing 3'

HABIT: Glossy foliage, large white flowers in early summer.
CULTURE: Needs highly organic soil with good drainage. Even moisture is important. Milorganite or manure in winter is a good idea. Chelated iron and soil acidifiers are often needed.
USES: Screen, specimen, accent, flower fragrance, container plant.
PROBLEMS: Aphids, scale, white flies, chlorosis.
NOTES: A good dwarf variety exists but has the same problems as the full size plant. Native to China.

HAWTHORN, INDIAN

Rhapiolepsis indica
rah-pee-oh-LEP-sis IN-dee-kah

Evergreen · Sun/Light Shade
Ht. 2'-5' Spread 3'-5'
Spacing 2'-3'

HABIT: Sizes of the varieties vary but is generally a small evergreen shrub. Blue-black berries in fall. White or pink spring flowers.
CULTURE: New varieties seem to be more healthy but all like well prepared, well drained beds.
USES: Mass, foundation planting, low border, spring color.
PROBLEMS: Leaf fungus and fireblight.
NOTES: Roundleaf Hawthorn *(R. ovata)* is a large growing white flowering variety. 'Clara' and 'Snow' are white flowering compact varieties. 'Spring Rapture' is a dark pink. 'Jack Evans' and 'Entrantress' are pink. Native to Korea and Japan.

HOLLY, BURFORD

Ilex cornuta 'Burfordii'
EYE-lex cor-NUTE-ah

Evergreen · Sun/Shade
Ht. 15' Spread 15'
Spacing 4'-8'

HABIT: Upright, hard, single-spined leaves and red berries in winter.
CULTURE: Any soil, any exposure, good drainage. Should not be sheared into hedge.
USES: Specimen shrub or small tree, background, screen or tall border.
PROBLEMS: Scale, chlorosis.
NOTES: Always buy full, bushy plants. Leggy bargains never fill in well. An interesting large leafed holly is *Ilex latafolia*. Other large growing hollies that do well here are 'Emily Brunner' and 'Mary Nell.' Native to China and Korea.

HOLLY, DWARF BURFORD

Ilex cornuta 'Burfordii Nana'
EYE-lex cor-NUTE-ah

Evergreen · Sun/Shade
Ht. 3'-5' Spread 3'-5'
Spacing 2'-3'

HABIT: Same characteristics as Burford Holly but smaller, more compact and lower growing.
CULTURE: Sun or shade, any soil with good drainage. Moderate water and fertilization.
USES: Medium height border, mass, screen or background.
PROBLEMS: Scale occasionally, chlorosis.
NOTES: 'Willowleaf is a close kin with the same characteristics but narrow leaves — excellent plant. 'Dazzler' is a good heavy-berried holly. Despite what you might have heard, 'Berries Jubilee' is a coarse plant and poor choice. 'Carrisa' is a compact, single pointed, wavy leaf holly. Cultivated.

HOLLY, DWARF CHINESE

Ilex cornuta 'Rotunda'
EYE-lex cor-NUTE-ah row-TON-dah

Evergreen - Sun/Shade
Ht. 18"-36" Spread 24"-36"
Spacing 18"-24"

HABIT:	Low growing, rounded, compact, very dense spiny foliage. No berries. 'Carrisa' is a crinkly leafed single spined close kin.
CULTURE:	Any well drained soil but good organic bed preparation is best. Moderate water and fertilizer needs. Best to prune late February or early March just before the new growth.
USES:	Low border, mass or barrier. People and pets won't walk through this plant but once. One of the best low growing evergreens for commercial use.
PROBLEMS:	Scale but not serious.
NOTES:	Avoid using at home if you like to work in your garden barefooted. The large Chinese Holly that the dwarf was bred from is a coarse, undesirable plant. Originally from China — the dwarf forms are cultivated.

HOLLY, DWARF YAUPON

Ilex vomitoria 'Nana'
EYE-lex vom-ee-TORE-ee-uh

Evergreen - Sun/Shade
Ht. 18"-36" Spread 24"-36"
Spacing 18"-24"

HABIT:	Rounded, compact, dense foliage, small shiny oval leaves. A very tidy plant. Flowers insignificant, no berries.
CULTURE:	Any soil, likes well prepared beds best. Seems to tolerate fairly wet soils but prefers good drainage.
USES:	Low border or mass planting.
PROBLEMS:	Leaf rollers occasionally.
NOTES:	This is the dwarf form of the Texas Native Yaupon Holly tree. New version called 'Soft Yaupon' is in my opinion still unproven as to hardiness here.

HOLLY, EAST PALATKA

Ilex x *attenuata* 'East Palatka'
EYE-lex ah-ten-you-AH-tah

Evergreen - Sun/Part Shade
Ht. 15'-30' Spread 10'-15'
Spacing 8'-10'

HABIT:	Large bush or small tree. Upright, moderate growth, rather open branching. Red berries in winter, smooth light bark.
CULTURE:	Any soil except solid rock, needs good drainage.
USES:	Specimen ornamental, evergreen border, small garden tree.
PROBLEMS:	Scale, mealy bugs, iron deficiency (none serious).
NOTES:	Distinguished by one spine on end of leaf rather than several like 'Savannah' and 'Fosteri.' All are hybrids of American Holly *(I. opaca)*.

HOLLY, FOSTER

Ilex x *attenuata* 'Fosteri'
EYE-lex ah-ten-you-AH-tah

Evergreen - Sun/Shade
Ht. 20' Spread 10'
Spacing 3'-10'

HABIT:	Small, dark-green spiny leaves, upright pyramidal growth, many small red berries in winter. Fairly slow growth.
CULTURE:	Relatively easy to grow in any well drained soil, prefers slightly acid soil but adapts well to alkaline clays.
USES:	Specimen evergreen tree, border or background plant, berry color in winter.
PROBLEMS:	Leaf miners occasionally.
NOTES:	Excellent plant for dark green color. Cultivated.

HOLLY, NELLIE R. STEVENS

Ilex x 'Nellie R. Stevens'
EYE-lex

Evergreen - Sun/Shade
Ht. 10'-20' Spread 10'-20'
Spacing 4'-14'

HABIT: Large, dark-green leaves and showy red berries in fall and winter. Spring flowers are insignificant. Extremely durable.

CULTURE: Will be more compact and healthy in full sun but can tolerate fairly heavy shade. Tolerates severe weather conditions.

USES: Screen or specimen plant. Can be trimmed into ornamental tree. Good in containers.

PROBLEMS: None. One of the most durable plants available.

NOTES: 'Nellie R. Stevens' is a cross between English Holly *(I. aquifolium)* and Chinese Holly *(I. cornuta)*.

HOLLY, SAVANNAH

Ilex opaca 'Savannah'
EYE-lex o-PAY-kuh

Evergreen - Sun/Shade
Ht. 15'-30' Spread 10'-15'
Spacing 8'-12'

HABIT: Moderate upright and pyramidal growth, medium green spiny leaves. Lots of red berries in winter.

CULTURE: Easy in any well drained soil.

USES: Small specimen garden tree, border or evergreen background.

PROBLEMS: Few, leaf miners occasionally.

NOTES: Good small evergreen tree. Cultivated. Is beginning to be used often.

HOLLY, WEEPING YAUPON

Ilex vomitoria 'Pendula'
EYE-lex vom-ee-TORE-ee-uh PEN-due-lah

Evergreen - Sun/Shade
Ht. 15'-20' Spread 8'-10'
Spacing 5'-10'

HABIT: Upright with sharply drooping limbs. Red berries on female plants in winter. Smaller leaves than regular Yaupon Holly.

CULTURE: Easy to grow in any well drained soil.

USES: Specimen garden ornamental, border, background plant, container tree, Oriental gardens.

PROBLEMS: Few if any.

NOTES: Very interesting and unusual plant. Native to southeast USA.

HONEYSUCKLE, WHITE (Native)

Lonicera albiflora
lon-ISS-er-uh al-bi-FLOOR-ah

Deciduous - Sun/Part Shade
Ht. 8'-10' Spread 8'-10'
Spacing 4'-8'

HABIT: Many stems from ground growing up and arching over to form a loosely shaped shrub. White flowers in spring, showy red berries in late summer and yellow fall color. Bare branches most of winter.

CULTURE: Easy, any soil, drought tolerant.

USES: Shrub mass for soft, natural effect.

PROBLEMS: A little wild looking for formal gardens. Otherwise no problems.

NOTES: This shrub exists on many properties around north Texas. Most people cut it down. I would try to keep it in many situations. Winter Honeysuckle *(L. fragrantissima)* has round leaves and flowers in winter. Both are native to Texas and Oklahoma.

HORSETAIL REED
Equisetum hyemale
eh-kwee-SEAT-um HIM-ah-lee

Perennial - Sun/Part Shade
Ht. 2'-4' Spread Unlimited
Spacing 18"

HABIT: Slender, hollow, vertical stems. Green with black rings at each joint.
CULTURE: Grows in soil or water. Does not need good drainage.
USES: Marshy or wet areas, bog gardens, aquatic gardens. Distinctive accent.
PROBLEMS: Will spread.
NOTES: Prehistoric plant, very interesting and easy to use. Native to Eurasia and the Pacific Northwest.

HOSTA
Hosta spp.
HOSS-tah

Perennial - Shade/Part Shade
Ht. 1'-3' Spread 2'-3'
Spacing 1'-3'

HABIT: Tufted, leafy plants. Fragrant white, lilac or blue spiked flowers in late summer. Many varieties and cultivars available.
CULTURE: Relatively easy. Moist, well drained soil. Can be divided in fall. Moderate fertilizer needs. Ample organic material in the soil is best.
USES: Mass or border for shade gardens. Used more for foliage than flowers.
PROBLEMS: Slugs, snails, heat of summer.
NOTES: Also called Plantain Lily or Shade Lily. Native to Korea, China and Japan. Those varieties with blue foliage like shade best, the variegated varieties like a little more sun but all do best with some shade. 'Royal Standard,' a large white flowered cultivar and 'Seiboldii' with lavender flowers are both excellent and immune to sunburn. No transplanting or division necessary.

HYDRANGEA
Hydrangea macrophylla
hi-DRAN-ja mac-crow-FILE-ah

Deciduous - Sun/Part Shade
Ht. 3'-5' Spread 3'-5'
Spacing 3'-4'

HABIT: Big, bold textured foliage and long lasting blue or pink flowers through the summer. Completely bare in winter.
CULTURE: Although shade loving, will produce more and larger flowers in bright places. Likes moist, richly organic soil best. Prune immediately after blooms fade away. Add acidifiers for blue flowers.
USES: Summer leaf texture and flower color.
PROBLEMS: None serious. Likes a lot of water.
NOTES: Should be used in association with evergreen plants. Native to Japan and China.

HYDRANGEA, OAK LEAF
Hydrangea quercifolia
hi-DRAN-ja kwer-si-FOAL-ee-ah

Deciduous - Sun/Part Shade
Ht. 6'-7' Spread 6'-8'
Spacing 3'-4'

HABIT: Good looking, coarse textured foliage that has excellent orange to reddish-purple fall color. Showy white flowers in late spring to early summer. The bare stems are even attractive in winter.
CULTURE: Easy to grow but likes well prepared beds that drain best.
USES: Great understory plants. Interesting texture, spring and fall color. Accent plant.
PROBLEMS: None.
NOTES: More deciduous shrubs should be used in general but this is one of the best. Native to Georgia, Mississippi and Florida.

HYPERICUM
Hypericum spp.
hi-PEAR-eh-cum

Evergreen · Sun/Part Shade
Ht. 2'-3' Spread 3'-4'
Spacing 18"-24"

HABIT:	Low growing, attractive foliage and showy yellow flowers in summer. Foliage is sometimes reddish in fall.
CULTURE:	Any soil, sun or part shade. Prepared beds, moderate water and food requirements.
USES:	Mass, accent, summer color.
PROBLEMS:	None.
NOTES:	Native to Europe. Several good varieties available. *H. pagulum henryi* is the most commonly used here. *Hypericum beani* is apparently the correct name.

JASMINE, ITALIAN
Jasminum humile
JAS-min-num HUME-eh-lee

Semi-evergreen · Sun
Ht. 5'-6' Spread 5'-6'
Spacing 3'-4'

HABIT:	Gracefully arching shrub with green stems and small yellow flowers in early summer. Loses half to two-thirds of its foliage in winter.
CULTURE:	Well prepared, well drained soil. Moderate water and fertilization needs. Little pruning needed. In fact, heavy clipping or shearing will ruin this plant.
USES:	Border, hedge.
PROBLEMS:	Freeze damage in harsh winters.
NOTES:	Native to China. *Jasminum nudiflorum,* a close kin, is completely deciduous.

JUNIPER, TAM
Juniperus sabina 'Tamariscifolia'
joo-NIP-er-us sa-BEAN-ah

Evergreen · Sun
Ht. 5' Spread 6'
Spacing 36"

HABIT:	Medium height, dark green foliage, dense to the ground.
CULTURE:	Needs open, well drained area, any soil, average water and fertilization.
USES:	Evergreen mass, tall groundcover. Good cold tolerance.
PROBLEMS:	Red spider and bagworms.
NOTES:	I prefer leafy shrubs that are more insect resistant.

LAUREL, CHERRY
Prunus caroliniana
PROO-nus ka-ro-lin-ee-AA-nah

Evergreen · Sun/Shade
Ht. 25' Spread 15'
Spacing 8'-15'

HABIT:	Upright bushy growth, can be trimmed into tree form. White flowers along stems in spring. 'Bright and Tight' is an improved compact cultivar.
CULTURE:	Will grow in any soil but is not long lived.
USES:	Evergreen screen, small ornamental.
PROBLEMS:	Borers, cotton root rot, crown gall, chlorosis and ice storms.
NOTES:	There are much better choices. Native eastern USA to Texas.

LAUREL, TEXAS MOUNTAIN (Native)

Sophora secundiflora
so-FORE-uh se-kune-di-FLOOR-uh

Evergreen - Sun/Part Shade
Ht. 20' Spread 10'
Spacing 8'-15'

HABIT:	Slow, dense foliage, bushy unless trimmed into tree form. Fragrant, purple, wisteria-like flowers in spring.
CULTURE:	Any well drained soil.
USES:	Specimen ornamental tree or large shrub. Drought tolerant gardens.
PROBLEMS:	Winter damage in the northern parts of the state.
NOTES:	Great in central Texas but not so hot in north Texas. Native to southwest USA, Texas and Mexico.

LIGUSTRUM, JAPANESE

Ligustrum lucidum
li-GUS-strum loo-SEE-dum

Evergreen - Sun/Part Shade
Ht. 15'-20' Spread 8'-10'
Spacing 4'-8'

HABIT:	Very large, vigorous shrub with larger, duller leaves than Wax Ligustrum. Clusters of blue berries in winter.
CULTURE:	Any soil, sun or part shade. Low water and fertilizer requirements.
USES:	Tall screen, ornamental tree.
PROBLEMS:	Cotton root rot, whiteflies and ice storm damage.
NOTES:	1983 freeze killed and severely damaged many of these plants. Native to the Orient. I try to keep this plant if existing on a site but seldom plant new ones.

LIGUSTRUM, VARIEGATED

Ligustrum luicidum 'Variegata'
li-GUS-trum loo-SEE-dum

Evergreen - Sun/Part Shade
Ht. 6'-10' Spread 6'-8'
Spacing 3'-4'

HABIT:	Small rounded leaves, dense branching. Light, variegated foliage.
CULTURE:	Easy, any soil, sun or part shade. Drought tolerant.
USES:	Color contrast, hedge or screen.
PROBLEMS:	None.
NOTES:	Often called variegated privet. Native to China and Korea.

LIGUSTRUM, WAX

Ligustrum japonicum
li-GUS-trum ja-PON-eh-cum

Evergreen - Sun/Part Shade
Ht. 10'-15' Spread 8'-10'
Spacing 3'-4'

HABIT:	Glossy leaves, blue berries in winter. Usually multi-trunked but single stem plants available at nurseries.
CULTURE:	Any soil and condition as long as drainage is good. Light shearing or pick pruning in March and July is helpful to keep the plant compact.
USES:	Ornamental tree, screen, tall border, background plant.
PROBLEMS:	Whiteflies, cotton root rot. Freeze damage in severe winters.
NOTES:	Waxleaf has been grossly misused as a foundation planting or low hedge. I also think pyramid, poodle and globe shaped pruning is a silly thing to do with this plant. Native to the Orient.

LOQUAT

Eriobotrya japonica
err-eh-o-BOT-tree-ah ja-PON-eh-cah

Evergreen · Sun/Part Shade
Ht. 10'-15' Spread 10'-15'
Spacing 8'-12'

HABIT: Large shrub or small tree. Large, leathery, grey-green leaves. Fragrant off-white flowers in fall and edible fruit in the spring.

CULTURE: Any soil with moderate water and fertilizer. Does best in well prepared beds in areas protected from winter winds.

USES: Screen, specimen or background plant. Lower foliage can be trimmed off to form small ornamental tree.

PROBLEMS: Fireblight (spray with streptomycin in fall when plant is in bloom). Freeze damage.

NOTES: Many loquats died in the 1983 freeze. Native to China and Japan.

MAHONIA, LEATHER LEAF

Mahnia bealei
mah-HONE-i-ah BEAL-ee-eye

Evergreen · Shade
Ht. 5'-7' Spread 3'-5'
Spacing 3'

HABIT: Unique shrub with vertical stems, thick spiny leaves, yellow early spring flowers and blue berries following. Tends to get leggy but that gives it the dramatic character.

CULTURE: Easy. Best in prepared beds in shade. Moderate water and food requirements. Remove one-third of the canes per year, if a more bushy effect is desired.

USES: Accent, distinctive foliage and character, Oriental gardens.

PROBLEMS: None.

NOTES: Native to China. The closely kin Oregon Grape *(Mahonia aquifolim)* is unsuccessful here despite what you may have heard. It needs a cooler climate such as its native home, the Pacific Northwest.

NANDINA

Nandina domestica
nan-DEE-nah doe-MESS-ti-ka

Evergreen · Sun/Shade
Ht. 12"-8' Spread 2'-6'
Spacing 2'-4'

HABIT: Vertical unbranching shoots, leggy but distinctive. Soft, delicate red-orange foliage and red berries in winter. Small white flowers in spring. Regular Nandina 5'-8', Compact 3'-4', Harbour Dwarf 1'-2' and 'Nana' 1'-2'.

CULTURE: Any soil, anywhere. Drought tolerant. Do not shear or box — ever! Can take an unbelievable amount of neglect. To lower height, cut the tallest shoots off at ground level.

USES: Specimen, container, accent, screen, hedge, Oriental gardens, mass, border.

PROBLEMS: None.

NOTES: Called Heavenly Bamboo. Nandinas, native to China, are just wonderful plants but have a curious negative connotation with many people. That's probably because they are seen growing wild around abandoned properties. All that really shows is how tough they are. All good except 'Nana'. It looks like a chlorotic basketball in summer.

Compact Nandina

Harbour Dwarf Nandina

Dwarf Nandina 'Nana'

OLEANDER
Nerium oleander
NEAR-ee-um oh-lee-AN-der

Evergreen - Sun
Ht. 8'-12' Spread 8'-12'
Spacing 5'-8'

HABIT: Upright shrub with many ascending stems that are bare below. Long thin leaves and red, white or pink flowers all summer long.

CULTURE: Plant in well prepared beds with protection from the winter winds.

USES: Screen, background, summer color.

PROBLEMS: Very poisonous plant parts, freeze damage.

NOTES: Hearty Red and Pink are the two most hearty here. 'Mrs. Roeding' is the gorgeous salmon color cultivar in the photo. It needs protection in harsh winters. Native to the Mediterranean.

PAMPAS GRASS
Cortaderia selloana
core-ta-DER-ee-ah sell-oh-AN-ah

Perennial - Sun
Ht. 8' Spread 8'
Spacing 8'-10'

HABIT: Fountain-like grass clump with long, slender, sharp edged blades of foliage. White flower plumes in late summer and last quite long into the winter. Foliage turns brown in harsh winter and should be cut back.

CULTURE: Easy in any soil. Low water and food requirements. Needs good drainage like most plants.

USES: Accent plant, border for roads, drives or parks. Good for distant viewing.

PROBLEMS: Few if any.

NOTES: White plumes are good for interior arrangements. Female plants have the showiest plumes. Native to South America. Muhlie Grass *(Muhlenbergia lindheimeri)* is similar but more natural looking and native to Texas.

PHOTINIA, CHINESE
Photinia serrulata
foe-TEN-ee-ah sir-roo-LA-ta

Evergreen - Sun/Part Shade
Ht. 15'-20' Spread 15'-20'
Spacing 5'-10'

HABIT: Massive, spreading evergreen shrub. Can be trimmed into small tree. Clusters of white flowers in spring and red berries in winter.

CULTURE: Any soil, low water and food requirements.

USES: Background, screen, small garden tree.

PROBLEMS: Poisonous, powdery mildew, aphids, borers, leaf spot and firebright.

NOTES: Native to China and Asia. Larger growing than Fraser's Photinia.

PHOTINIA, FRASER'S
Photinia x 'fraseri'
foe-TEN-ee-ah FRAY-ser-eye

Evergreen - Sun/Part Shade
Ht. 10'-15' Spread 8'-10'
Spacing 4'-6'

HABIT: Very colorful, multi-stemmed, upright oval in shape. New growth in spring is red. No flowers or berries.

CULTURE: Likes well drained, prepared beds. Avoid wet soils. Drainage is critical.

USES: Screen, background, spring color. Foliage makes good cut flower material.

PROBLEMS: Poisonous, grossly overused. When the Wax Ligustrum froze in 1983, everyone replaced with Photinia. Root fungus problem and nitrogen deficiency.

NOTES: Also called Red Tip Photinia, a cross between Chinese Photinia *(P. serrulata)* and Japanese Photinia *(P. glabra)* which is a smaller growing plant. Cultivated. Root fungus problems are quite significant and sometimes strike after the plant has been healthy for 7 or 8 years.

PINE, MUGHO

Pinus mugo 'Mughus'
PIE-nus MEW-go MEW-gus

Evergreen - Sun
Ht. 4' Spread 4'
Spacing 3'-4'

HABIT: Shrubby, symmetrical little pine which becomes spreading with age.
CULTURE: Needs loose, well drained soil. Likes sandy, acid soil best. Seems to adapt to alkaline soil fairly well.
USES: Specimen, accent, Oriental gardens, containers.
PROBLEMS: Heat, chlorosis, pine tip moth.
NOTES: Chelated iron (Sequestrene) can help greatly to keep Mugho Pine healthy. Native to central and southern Europe.

PITTOSPORUM, VARIEGATED

Pittosporum tobira 'Variegata'
pit-tos-SPOR-um toe-BY-rah

Evergreen - Sun/Part Shade
Ht. 6'-7' Spread 5'-6'
Spacing 36"

HABIT: Soft, billowy-shaped shrub. Gray-green foliage edged in white. Although will grow much taller, can be kept trimmed to a 36" height.
CULTURE: Plant in well prepared and drained beds with protection against the winter winds. Moderate water and foods needs.
USES: Foundation, mass, tall border, cut flower foliage.
PROBLEMS: Severe freeze damage.
NOTES: Although the 1983 freeze killed almost every Pittosporum in north Texas, people are still planting them. I do not advise using them. Solid green form exists and has the same characteristics.

PITTOSPORUM, WHEELER'S DWARF

Pittosporum tobira 'Wheeler's Dwarf'
pit-tos-SPOR-um toe-BY-rah

Evergreen - Sun/Part Shade
Ht. 3'-4' Spread 3'-4'
Spacing 24"

HABIT: Very low, dense and compact. Available in green or variegated form. Same soft foliage as the full size variety.
CULTURE: Plant in well prepared and drained beds with good protection from north winds.
USES: Low border, mass or foundation plant.
PROBLEMS: Pittosporums can freeze easily.
NOTES: Limbs are easily broken by pets and kids.

PODOCARPUS

Podocarpus macrophyllus
po-doe-CAR-pus mac-crow-FILE-us

Evergreen - Shade/Part Shade
Ht. 10'-15' Spread 4'-6'
Spacing 3'-4'

HABIT: Vertical growing shrub with dark green foliage and blue berries in winter.
CULTURE: Plant in well prepared bed. Needs excellent drainage. Moderate food.
USES: Specimen, background plant, screen.
PROBLEMS: Root rot, nematodes.
NOTES: Also called False Japanese Yew. *P. sinensis* is short and bushy and very cold hearty.

POMEGRANATE

Punica granatum
PEW-ni-kah gran-NAY-tum

Deciduous - Sun/Part Shade
Ht. 10'-15' Spread 8'-10'
Spacing 6'-8'

HABIT: Upright, many stems. Showy red-orange flowers in summer and yellow fall color. Narrow, glossy leaves, bronze new growth.
CULTURE: Any soil, anywhere. Quite tolerant of our soil and heat. Full sun for best blooms. Drought tolerant.
USES: Specimen, barrier, summer color.
PROBLEMS: Few if any.
NOTES: Like other deciduous flowering shrubs, the Pomegranate has not been used enough. Several improved cultivars exist — 'Albescens' is a white flowering selection. Native to Europe and Asia.

PYRACANTHA

Pyracantha spp.
pie-ra-CAN-tha

Evergreen - Sun
Ht. 3'-15' Spread 3'-15'
Spacing 4'-8'

HABIT: Large sprawling, viney, thorny shrub. White flowers in spring, red or orange berries in fall and winter. Can grow free form as a shrub or be trained to wall or fence.
CULTURE: Likes well prepared and drained beds. Good positive drainage is critical. Needs careful pruning to control growth. Consistent fertilization is important.
USES: Barrier, screen or mass planting.
PROBLEMS: Aphids, scale, lacebugs, mealy bugs, red spider, root rot.
NOTES: Also called Firethorn. Dwarf forms are available and are better for mass planting. I do not really recommend any of them. Many have died out around the state. Native to Europe and Asia.

QUINCE, FLOWERING

Chaenomeles japonica
key-NOM-me-lees ja-PON-eh-cah

Deciduous - Sun/Shade
Ht. 4'-6' Spread 4'-6'
Spacing 3'-4'

HABIT: First shrub to bloom each year in late winter. Flowers are various shades of red, pink and white.
CULTURE: Best in prepared beds but tolerates a wide range of soils. Will grow in sun or shade but blooms better in sun. Relatively drought tolerant.
USES: Spring flower display.
PROBLEMS: Leaf spot, chlorosis, heat.
NOTES: I use this plant more as a source of cut flowers than as a shrub since it looks so bad in the summer months. Native to China. Common Flowering Quince *(C. speciosa)* is the larger growing variety.

RHODODENDRON

Rhododendron spp.
row-do-DEN-dron

Evergreen - Shade/Part Shade
Ht. 3'-8' Spread 4'-8'
Spacing 3'-7'

HABIT: Larger and darker green leaves than azalea. Large showy flowers of red, pink, white, purple, yellow and orange in spring. Long lived shrub having at least 800 species. Some are tiny plants just inches tall, others grow to be trees 50'-60' tall.
CULTURE: Best in acid soil and cool moist climates so growing them here is tricky. Plant them in a 50-50 mix of peat moss and shredded bark or other coarse material. Drainage is critical. Shade, especially from afternoon sun, is important. Avoid dense, heavy shade. Feed with organic fertilizer only.
USES: Evergreen hedge, background plant or mass. Spring flower display.
PROBLEMS: Heat, low humidity. Avoid hot reflected light locations. Acid treating the irrigation water is needed in areas.
NOTES: Do not plant near shallow rooted trees. Root competition will be a problem. Around 5,000 hybrids at least. Native to Asia, North America, and the East Indies.

SAGE, TEXAS (Native)
Leucophyllum frutescens
lew-co-FI-lum FRU-tes-sens

Evergreen — Sun
Ht. 5'-7' Spread 5'-7'
Spacing 3'

HABIT:	Compact, soft and slow growing. Silver gray foliage. Purple or white flowers in summer. Will grow better if not overwatered.
CULTURE:	Any soil with good drainage. Drought and heat tolerant.
USES:	Specimen, mass, summer color, gray foliage.
PROBLEMS:	Too much water.
NOTES:	'Compactum' is the dwarf form, 'Green Cloud' has darker foliage and 'White Cloud' has white flowers. Native to Texas and Mexico.

SANTOLINA, GRAY
Santolina chamaecyparissus
san-toe-LINE-ah kam-ah-sip-eh-RIS-us

Evergreen - Sun
Ht. 12'-18' Spread 24'
Spacing 18'-24'

HABIT:	Low, compact and spreading. Herb-like foliage that is fragrant when crushed.
CULTURE:	Drought tolerant and not demanding except for needing excellent drainage.
USES:	Low border, mass, rock gardens, extremely hot, dry places.
PROBLEMS:	Poor drainage, too much water, red spider mites.
NOTES:	Also a dark green variety *(S. virens)* with the same characteristics. Native to Europe. Also called Lavender Cotton.

SMOKETREE
Cotinus coggyria
co-TEN-us cog-JEER-ee-ah

Deciduous - Sun/Part Shade
Ht. 10'-15' Spread 10'-15'
Spacing 6'-8'

HABIT:	Upright and open, beautiful round leaves. Several cultivars are available with a wide range of yellow, red and purple spring, summer and fall colors. Smoke-like false flowers in mid-summer.
CULTURE:	Tough plant, any soil, drought tolerant. Needs excellent drainage.
USES:	Specimen, foliage color, unique flowers.
PROBLEMS:	Few if any in well drained soil.
NOTES:	(syn. *Rhus cotinus*) Native to Europe and Asia. Two good purple leaf cultivars are 'Royal Purple' and 'Velvet Cloak.' Related to the American Smoketree best used for its spectacular fall color.

SPIREA
Spirea spp.
spy-REE-ah

Deciduous - Sun/Part Shade
Ht. 5'-7' Spread 6'-8'
Spacing 3'-5'

HABIT:	Rounded overall form, many stems from the ground, showy white or coral flowers in spring. Minimal fall color. Many good species and cultivars.
CULTURE:	Extremely tough plant that will grow anywhere.
USES:	Specimen, accent, screen, white spring flowers.
PROBLEMS:	None.
NOTES:	Landscape snobs think spirea is old fashioned — I think they are missing out on a great plant. 'Vanhouttei' spirea is a cross between two spireas from China. *S. bumalda* 'Anthony Waterer' is a beautiful coral-color flower that blooms later in the spring. Double Reeves Spirea *(S. cantoniensis* 'Lanceata') is another excellent choice. Native to Asia.

SUMAC, AROMATIC (Native)

Rhus aromatica
RUSE err-o-MAT-eh-kuh

Deciduous - Sun/Part Shade
Ht. 4'-6' Spread 5'-7'
Spacing 3'-4'

HABIT: Leaves have three leaflets which are fragrant when crushed. Plant will sucker and spread but usually not a problem. Yellow flowers in early spring followed by red berries. Red-orange fall color. Can grow as high as 12'.

CULTURE: Grows in any soil that has good drainage, even in rock. Fibrous roots, easy to transplant.

USES: Naturalizing an area. Attracts birds.

PROBLEMS: None.

NOTES: Also called Skunkbush and Fragrant Sumac. A good place to see this and other natives is the nature trail at Mountain View College. 'Gro-Low' is a compact form. 'Green Glove' is a larger cultivar. Native eastern USA to Texas.

SUMAC, FLAMELEAF (Native)

Rhus copallina
RUSE ko-pal-LINE-ah

Deciduous - Sun/Shade
Ht. 15' Spread 15'
Spacing 5'-10'

HABIT: Small, open growing tree. Leafy wings along stems. Brilliant red fall color. Seed clusters in winter. Spreads by suckers.

CULTURE: Easy, any soil. Can be bare rooted and likes little water.

USES: Specimen garden tree or background mass.

PROBLEMS: None except overwatering. Overwatering is sure to kill.

NOTES: Also called Shining Sumac because the top of the leaf is dark green and shiny above and hairy below. Prairie Flameleaf Sumac is *Rhus lanceolata.*

SUMAC, EVERGREEN (Native)

Rhus virens
RUSE VIE-rens

Evergreen - Sun
Ht. 7' Spread 7'
Spacing 3'-4'

HABIT: Bushy growth. Rounded leaves do not look like other sumacs. Red berries in summer. Reddish-purple fall color.

CULTURE: Drought tolerant and carefree. May need some protection from winter winds in north Texas. Overwatering is sure to kill.

USES: Specimen, mass planting, natural areas.

PROBLEMS: Possible freeze damage.

NOTES: Native to central Texas. Deer love this plant.

SUMAC, SMOOTH (Native)

Rhus glabra
RUSE GLA-bra

Deciduous - Sun/Part Shade
Ht. 10' Spread 10'
Spacing 4'-8'

HABIT: Thick stems with foliage at ends, spreads by suckers out from the mother plant. Excellent orange to red fall color. Vertical flowers and fruit which matures by fall and remains on bare stems through the winter.

CULTURE: Unbelievably durable and widely adaptable. Can be transplanted easily — even bare root. Can take more water than the other sumacs.

USES: Background, mass, natural areas, fall color.

PROBLEMS: Spreads.

NOTES: 'Lancinata' is a cut leaf cultivar that is almost fern-like.

VIBURNUM, JAPANESE
Viburnum odoratissimum
vi-BURN-um oh-doe-ra-TISS-eh-mum

Evergreen - Sun/Shade
Ht. 10' Spread 5'-7'
Spacing 4'-6'

HABIT:	Upright growth on thick stems. Large glossy leaves turning a slight bronze color in fall. Bushy but can be trimmed into a tree form.
CULTURE:	Well prepared and drained bed, moderate water and food needs.
USES:	Specimen, screen, background. Foliage is wonderful cut flower material. It is long lasting — in fact, it will easily root in water.
PROBLEMS:	Freeze damage.
NOTES:	This plant is often sold as *Viburnam macrophyllum*. *V. macrocephalum* is Chinese Snowball. *V. burkwoodi* is an excellent semi-evergreen. *V. caricephalum* is the Fragrant Viburnam. 'Spring Bouquet' is smaller growing evergreen cultivar.

YUCCA, HARD
Yucca aloifolia
YUCK-ah al-oh-eh-FOAL-ee-ah

Evergreen - Sun
Ht. 8'-10' Spread 8'-10'
Spacing 6'-8'

HABIT:	Dangerously stiff leaves. Attractive white flower cluster in early summer.
CULTURE:	Sun, any soil, drainage and very little water.
USES:	Desert-type gardens, specimen, accent.
PROBLEMS:	Sharp spiny leaves are very dangerous.
NOTES:	Handle with care and do not use where children might be playing. Native to the southern United States.

YUCCA, RED (Native)
Hesperaloe parviflora
hess-per-RAY-low par-vi-FLOOR-ah

Evergreen - Sun
Ht. 3' Spread 3'-5'
Spacing 3'-4'

HABIT:	Slender, fountain-like blue green foliage that is fairly slow growing. Reddish pink flowers bloom almost all summer.
CULTURE:	Extremely drought tolerant, any soil as long as it is well drained. Low food needs.
USES:	Specimen, accent, summer color.
PROBLEMS:	None.
NOTES:	Native to west Texas.

YUCCA, SOFT
Yucca gloriosa
YUCK-ah glor-ee-OH-sa

Evergreen - Sun
Ht. 3'-8' Spread 3'-4'
Spacing 3'-4'

HABIT:	Single unbranching trunk. Spreads by offshoots to make new plants. White flower stalk in summer.
CULTURE:	Any soil as long as well drained.
USES:	Accent or dramatic mass.
PROBLEMS:	None.
NOTES:	Looks best at height of 24"-36". When leggy it is best to cut off the tall part and let the baby plants take over. Native to southern United States.

GROUNDCOVER, VINES
GRASSES AND HERBS

EASY REFERENCE FOR
GROUNDCOVER, VINES, GRASSES AND HERBS

GROUNDCOVER

FOR SUN

Glauca Grass
Honeysuckle
Houttuynia
Jasmine, Asian
Juniper, Creeping
Liriope
Ophiopogon
Potentilla
Sedum
Thyme, Creeping
Vinca Minor
Wintercreeper

FOR SHADE

Houttuynia
Ivy, English
Jasmine, Asian
Lamium
Liriope
Moneywort
Ophiopogon
Pachysandra
Potentilla
Gill Ivy

VINES

FOR SUN

Bougainvillea
Clematis
Crossvine
Grape
Honeysuckle
Ivy, Boston
Ivy, Fig
Jasmine, Confederate
Jessamine, Carolina
Lacevine, Silver
Mandevilla
Morning Glory
Passion Vine
Rose, Lady Bank's
Trumpet Vine
Virginia Creeper
Wisteria

FOR SHADE

Clematis
Fatshedra
Ivy, Boston
Ivy, English
Ivy, Fig
Jasmine, Confederate
Virginia Creeper

RECOMMENDED HERBS

Artemesia
Basil
Bay
Curry
Dill
Garlic
Scented Geraniums

Lamb's Ear
Lamium
Mexican Mint Marigold
Mint
Onion Chives
Oregano
Parsley
Rosemary

Rue
Sage
Salad Burnett
Tansy
Thyme
Lemon Verbena
Yarrow

GRASSES

FOR SUN

Bermudagrass
Tifgrass
Buffalograss
St. Augustinegrass
Zoysiagrass

FOR SHADE

Fescue
St. Augustinegrass

GROUNDCOVER, VINES, GRASSES AND HERBS

Artemesia (*Artemesia* spp.) — Lacy, silver-gray herb grown for its ornamental foliage as well as its culinary and medicinal properties.

Basil (*Ocinum basilicum*) — A favorite culinary herb but also a good landscape plant. Many varieties and cultivars.

Bougainvillea (*Bougainvillea* spp.) — Tropical vine with vibrant summer colors. Use as an annual or overwinter indoors. Likes to dry out between waterings and cussing it occasionally makes it bloom better.

Silver Mound Dahlia (*Dahlia greggi*) — is a gray leaf groundcover-like perennial, bare in winter. Carefree, drought tolerant and great fun.

Gill Ivy (*Glechoma hederacea*) — Also called Ground Ivy, a most carefree but invasive groundcover, rounded leaves, grows in any soil in shade. Small purple flowers in spring.

Golden Vine (*Mascagnia macroptera*) — Bright yellow flower clusters cover this vine throughout the summer.

Gourds — Ornamental summer vine. Annual, plant from seed in spring. Easy and great fun.

Jew, Purple (*Zebrina pendula*) — Viney groundcover perennial with purple stems and leaves and small pink flowers in early summer.

Kudzu (*Pueraria lobata*) — Large leaves. Purple summer flowers. Called Jack and the Beau. Extremely rampant. Illegal in some states.

Lavender (*Lavandula* spp.) — English Lavender is *L. augustifolia*. 'Mumstead' is evergreen in mild winters. Makes a wonderful landscape plant.

Lovegrass, Weeping (*Eragrostis ehmanniana*) — Tall decorative grass 1'-2' in height. Foliage spills over in a weeping effect. Plant from seed in the spring.

Marigold, Mexican Mint (*Tagetes lucida*) — Perennial herb for sun or partial shade, dark green leaves. A substitute herb for French Tarragon. Marigold-like yellow flowers in fall.

Morning Glory (*Ipomoea* spp.) — Easy to grow from seed, likes poor soil, can be invasive. Moon Flower (*I. alba*) has large white blossoms that open at night.

Mint (*Mentha* spp.) — Herbs that can be used as groundcover. Most are fast growing and invasive. All have square stems. Spearmint (*M. spicata*), Peppermint (*M. piperita*), Orangemint (*M. citrata*). Corsican mint (*M. requieni*) is small leafed creeping variety that makes a good groundcover for small areas. Pennyroyal (*M. pulegium*) is also a low-growing form that repels fleas and mosquitos.

Oregano, Mexican (*Poliomintha longifolia*) — Sun or part shade. Shrub-like, small glossy leaves on woody stems. Perennial or semi-evergreen. Lavender blooms spring and summer.

Rue (*Ruta graveolens*) — Perennial herb with beautiful blue-green foliage that can cause dermatitis in some people.

Vetch, Crown (*Coronilla varia*) — Sprawling vine-like herb, purplish flowers in early summer. Best for groundcover on steep, rocky, hard to maintain areas in full sun. Plant from seed in spring. Can be invasive.

AJUGA

Ajuga reptans 'Atropurpurea'
ah-JOO-ga REP-tans

Evergreen - Shade
Ht. 3"-6" Ground Cover
Spacing 6"-9"

HABIT:	Low growing, spread by runners. Bronzy-purple leaves and purple flowers on short stalks.
CULTURE:	Well prepared beds with good drainage. Fairly high water and fertilizer requirements.
USES:	Ground cover for small areas.
PROBLEMS:	Nematodes are a real problem.
NOTES:	Do not invest much money in this plant. It's pretty when healthy but rarely is. Native to Europe.

BERMUDAGRASS, COMMON

Cynodon dactylon
SIN-no-don DAC-ti-lon

Warm season - Sun
Mowing Ht. 1½"
Seed @ 2 lbs. per 1000 s.f.

HABIT:	Narrow leaf blade, spread by stolons and rhizomes. Brown in winter.
CULTURE:	Low maintenance, aggressive grass. Grows in any soil. Does much better with ample water and food but is quite drought tolerant. Does not develop thatch.
USES:	Lawn grass, playing fields.
PROBLEMS:	Some insects and diseases but none serious.
NOTES:	Mixing with St. Augustine and some weeds looks OK. Native to warm regions around the world. Grass planting around new shrubs and trees will retard their growth. Texturf-10 is a dark green variety, relatively free of seed stems and a good choice for athletic fields.

BERMUDAGRASS, TIF (TIFGRASS)

Cynodon dactylon Cultivars
SIN-no-don DAC-ti-lon

Warm season - Sun
Mowing Ht. 1/2" - 3/4"
Stolons @ 10-15 bushels/1000 s.f.

HABIT:	Hybrid forms of Common Bermudagrass. Narrower leaf blade and finer overall texture. Tifdwarf is the finest textured, Tifgreen 328 is slightly larger, and Tifway 419 is the largest and is the best of the hybrids for residential use.
CULTURE:	Higher maintenance since weeds and imperfections are much more visible.
USES:	Refined lawns and putting greens. Also golf course tees and fairways. These grasses are sterile (no seeds) and must be planted solid or from stolons.
PROBLEMS:	Some insects and diseases but none serious. Bad thatch build up.
NOTES:	Too much work for home lawns. Native to laboratory.

BUFFALOGRASS (Native)

Buchloe dactyloides
BUCK-low dac-ti-LOY-dees

Warm season - Sun
Mowing Ht. 2"-3"
Seed @ 5 lbs./1000 s.f.

HABIT:	Low growing, blue green foliage, decorative flag-like flower heads — that most people think are the seeds — on the male plants.
CULTURE:	Easy, any soil except wet areas. Plant from seed in spring (through September if irrigated).
USES:	Lawn grass, large natural areas, low maintenance.
PROBLEMS:	Slow to establish is more an adjustment than a problem.
NOTES:	Our only native lawn grass and the most drought tolerant and low maintenance grass of all. Fertilize only once with initial seeding. Do not water too much. Native from Texas to Minnesota and Montana.

CLEMATIS, FALL
Clematis paniculata
KLEM-ah-tis pa-NICK-you-la-ta

Perennial - Sun/Shade
Vine
Spacing 3'-6'

HABIT: Vigorous semi-evergreen climbing vine with profusion of fragrant 1" white flowers in the late summer.

CULTURE: Easy in any well drained soil. Low to moderate water and light fertilizer needs. Don't prune the first year.

USES: Climbing vine for fences, arbors and decorative screens. Late summer flower color.

PROBLEMS: Somewhat aggressive.

NOTES: Correct botanical name is *C. maximowieziana*. Also called Sweet Autumn Clematis. Native to Japan. *Clematis* 'Jackaranda' also does pretty well here in filtered light. Scarlet Clematis *(Clematis texensis)* is native and has small unusual red flowers.

CROSSVINE (Native)
Bignonia capreolata
big-NONE-ee-uh kap-ree-o-LATE-uh

Evergreen - Sun/Part Shade
Vine
Spacing 4'-8'

HABIT: Climbs by tendrils and has unusual yellow and red flower in the spring.

CULTURE: Any soil, sun or shade. Moderate water and fertilization. Easy to control.

USES: Vine for fences, overhead structures, and decorative screens.

PROBLEMS: Few if any.

NOTES: Interesting vine to use because it hasn't been used much. Native southern USA to Texas.

FESCUE, TALL
Festuca spp.
fess-TOO-cah

Cool season - Sun/Shade
Mowing Ht. 2"
Seed @ 8-10 lbs./1000 s.f.

HABIT: Bunch type grass that is planted as a winter overseeding or used in shady lawn areas. A permanent grass.

CULTURE: Needs fertile well drained soil and should be planted in the fall (Sept.-Nov.) for best results.

USES: Lawn grass in shade, overseeding.

PROBLEMS: Have to mow all winter, looks somewhat artificial in north Texas.

NOTES: Best of the winter grasses for home use. Native to Europe. Ryegrass and Roughstalk Bluegrass are often used as an overseed grass, however they are very competitive in the spring with the permanent grasses.

GLAUCA GRASS
Festuca ovina 'Glauca'
fess-TOO-kah oh-VEEN-uh GLAH-kah

Evergreen - Sun
Ht. 4"-10" Groundcover
Spacing 9"-12"

HABIT: Slender, bristly, powdery blue-gray, hair-like leaves forming distinct clumps. Light colored flowers on thin stalks in early spring.

CULTURE: Easy to grow in any soil, drought tolerant and low fertilization needs. Clip away flowers after the blooms have faded.

USES: Groundcover or low border.

PROBLEMS: Never grows in real solid, so mulching is important to prevent weeds.

NOTES: Also called Blue Fescue Grass. Native to southeast Asia and Japan.

GRAPE

Vitis spp.
VIE-tis

Deciduous · Sun
Vine
Spacing 8'-10'

HABIT: Fast growing climber for trellis or overhead structure. Needs support to get started.
CULTURE: Any well drained soil, low water and fertilization requirements.
USES: Good for quickly cooling a hot spot in summer. Grapes.
PROBLEMS: Grasshoppers, caterpillars, Pierce's Disease on 'Concord' and 'Thompson Seedless.' Try to buy other varieties.
NOTES: Some grape vines can get out of hand by growing so fast. Keep them out of trees. Native worldwide. The native 'Wild Mustang' is great for jams and jellies.

HONEYSUCKLE

Lonicera japonica 'Atropurpurea'
lon-ISS-er-uh ja-PON-eh-cah

Evergreen · Sun/Part Shade
Ht 12"-20" Vine or Groundcover
Spacing 12" (G.C.) 6' Vine

HABIT: Aggressive climbing vine or groundcover. Needs support at first to climb. Fragrant white and yellow blooms. Tends to get leggy.
CULTURE: Any soil, anywhere. Very drought tolerant.
USES: Unrefined groundcover areas. Erosion control of slopes.
PROBLEMS: Too aggressive and invasive. Chokes out more desirable plants.
NOTES: There are several choices better than Honeysuckle but it exists in many places, so we have to deal with it. Native to Asia and the Orient.

HONEYSUCKLE, CORAL (Native)

Lonicera sempervirens
lon-ISS-er-uh sem-per-VYE-rens

Evergreen · Sun
Vine
Spacing 3'-8'

HABIT: Climbing vine that needs support to start. Coral-red flowers all summer.
CULTURE: Any soil, drought tolerant but does better with irrigation.
USES: Climbing vine for fences, walls, arbors and decorative screens.
PROBLEMS: Few if any.
NOTES: Good plant for attracting hummingbirds. *L. sempervirens* 'Sulphurea' is a beautiful yellow flowering variety. Native eastern USA to Texas.

HOUTTUYNIA

Houttuynia cordata 'Variegata'
who-TEEN-yah core-DAH-tah

Perennial · Sun/Shade
Ht. 1' Groundcover
Spacing 1'-2'

HABIT: Colorful groundcover that spreads aggressively and has yellow rosy and red foliage color in full sun.
CULTURE: Can take any soil condition but does best in wet or boggy soil.
USES: Groundcover for poorly drained areas.
PROBLEMS: Needs to be contained. Can be invasive.
NOTES: A nice surprise — loves wet feet. Bruised foliage smells like citrus. Native to Japan. Dies completely away in winter.

IVY, BOSTON
Parthenocissus tricuspidata 'Lowii'
par-then-oh-SIS-us try-cus-pi-DA-tah

Deciduous · Sun/Shade
Vine
Spacing 6'-8'

HABIT: Fast growing, clinging vine. No showy flowers, but fall color that ranges from weak reddish-brown to bright scarlet.
CULTURE: Easy to grow most anywhere. Likes good bed preparation and partial shade best.
USES: Vine for brick, wood or other slick surfaces.
PROBLEMS: Black caterpillars in spring.
NOTES: Native to China and Japan. 'Beverly Brooks' is the large leaf plant and 'Lowii' is the small leafed plant that I prefer.

IVY, ENGLISH
Hedera helix
HEAD-eh-rah HE-lix

Evergreen · Shade/Part Shade
Ht. 1'-50' Vine and Groundcover
Spacing 12" (G.C.) 4' (Vine)

HABIT: Relatively fast growing vine for north exposure or other shady spot. Excellent ground-cover for shade or partial shade. Will climb any surface.
CULTURE: Needs good bed preparation, good drainage and mulch for establishment. Keep trimmed from windows, eaves and the canopy of trees.
USES: Groundcover for shade and part sun, vine for shade.
PROBLEMS: Aphids, cotton root rot, leaf spot, root and stem fungus.
NOTES: Plant used as groundcover should be trimmed back in late winter/early spring just like all groundcovers but with more care. 'Needlepoint' and 'Hahns' ivy are smaller leafed cultivars. 'Wilsoni' is a crinkled leaf choice. Native to Europe, Asia and Africa. *Fatshreda* is a vine cross between English Ivy and *Fatsia Japonica.*

IVY, FIG
Ficus pumila
FIE-cus PEW-mi-lah

Evergreen · Sun/Shade
Vine
Spacing 3'-5'

HABIT: Small leafed climbing vine that needs no support. Climbs by aerial roots.
CULTURE: Prefers a moist, well drained soil and high humidity. Needs protection from winter winds. Sunny southern exposure is best.
USES: Climbing vine for protected courtyards, conservatories and garden rooms.
PROBLEMS: Freeze damage in severe winters.
NOTES: Also called Climbing or Creeping Fig. Native to southeast Asia and Japan.

JASMINE, ASIAN
Trachelospermum asiaticum
tray-kell-o-SPER-mum aa-she-AT-ti-cum

Evergreen · Sun/Shade
Ht. 6"-12" Groundcover
Spacing 12"

HABIT: Dense, low growing groundcover that will climb but not readily. Small oval leaves, no flowers. A variegated form and a dwarf called 'Elegans' now exist.
CULTURE: Needs moist, well drained, well prepared soil for establishment. Once established, fairly drought tolerant. Cut down by mowing at highest setting in late winter — again in July if wanted.
USES: Groundcover for large areas.
PROBLEMS: Extreme winters can severely damage or kill this plant. Average winters will often burn the foliage brown, but recovers in spring.
NOTES: Also called Japanese Star Jasmine and Asiatic Jasmine. Native to Japan and Korea. If any of your Asian Jasmine has flowers, it's the wrong plant — either Confederate or Yellow Star Jasmine.

JASMINE, CONFEDERATE
Trachelospermum jasminoides
tray-kell-lo-SPER-mum jazz-min-OY-dees

Evergreen · Sun/Shade
Vine
Spacing 3'-5'

HABIT: Fast, open growing, climbing vine, dark green leaves, white flowers in summer. Will bloom in sun or shade. Requires support to climb.
CULTURE: Well prepared and well drained beds. Moderate water and fertilizer needs. Freezes fairly often — best to treat as an annual.
USES: Climbing vine for fence, trellis, pole or decorative screen.
PROBLEMS: Freeze damage.
NOTES: I usually treat this plant like an annual and just plant another if it freezes. Yellow Jasmine *(T. mandaianum)* is lemon scented and more cold tolerant.

JESSAMINE, CAROLINA
Gelsemium sempervirens
jel-SEE-mee-um sem-per-VYE-rens

Evergreen · Sun
Vine
Spacing 4'-8'

HABIT: Climbing vine that needs support to start. Profuse yellow flowers in the early spring. Will sometimes bloom during warm spells in winter — no problem.
CULTURE: Well prepared soil, good drainage, moderate water and fertilizer. Top of plant sometimes needs thinning to prevent a large mass from forming. Will grow in shade but not bloom well.
USES: Climbing vine in full sun for arbors, fences, walls, screens. Early spring color. Should not be used as a groundcover.
PROBLEMS: None.
NOTES: Is not a Jasmine. All parts of plant are poisonous, but not to the touch. Native to east Texas, Florida and Virginia.

JUNIPER, CREEPING
Juniperus horizontalis
joo-NIP-er-us hor-eh-zon-TALL-us

Evergreen · Sun
Ht. 1'-2' Spread 3'-6'
Spacing 18"-24"

HABIT: Low spreading juniper that acts like a groundcover. 'Bar Harbour' is blue green in summer with a nice purple color in the winter. 'Wiltoni' (Blue Rug) is silver-blue in summer with a light purple cast in winter. Dozens of other varieties.
CULTURE: Well prepared, well drained soil. Drought tolerant, although responds well to even moisture and regular fertilization.
USES: Groundcover for hot areas, raised planters.
PROBLEMS: Red spider mites, juniper blight.
NOTES: Shore Juniper is also a low growing juniper with soft, light green foliage. Native to Nova Scotia, Canada, northern United States.

LACEVINE, SILVER
Polygonum aubertii
poe-LIG-eh-num awe-BERT-ee-eye

Deciduous · Sun
Vine
Spacing 4'-8'

HABIT: Fast growing, climbing vine, spreads by rhizomes. Twining character. Small white flowers in summer.
CULTURE: Easy to grow, drought tolerant and low fertilizer requirements.
USES: Climbing vine for hot dry areas, summer flower color.
PROBLEMS: Can be aggressive and weed-like.
NOTES: Native to China.

LAMIUM

Lamium maculatum 'Variegatum'
LAM-ee-um mac-you-LAY-tum

Perennial · Shade/Part Shade
Ht. 9"-12" Groundcover
Spacing 9"-12"

HABIT:	Low growing, silvery leafed groundcover, spreads easily. Flowers purple, red or white in summer.
CULTURE:	Easy, any well drained soil. Moderate water and fertilizer. Needs afternoon shade. Does best in moist soil.
USES:	Groundcover, containers.
PROBLEMS:	Fairly carefree.
NOTES:	Also called Spotted Dead Nettle. 'White Nancy' is a nice white cultivar. Several other improved cultivars exist.

LIRIOPE

Liriope muscari
la-RYE-oh-pee MUS-ca-rye

Evergreen · Sun/Shade
Ht. 9"-15" Groundcover
Spacing 12"

HABIT:	Grass-like clumps that spread by underground stems to form solid mass planting. Has primarily one flush of growth in the spring. Blue flowers on stalks in early summer.
CULTURE:	Easy to grow in well prepared beds that drain well. Does best in shade or partial shade. Mow or clip down to 3" in late winter just before the new spring growth. Easy to divide and transplant anytime.
USES:	Low border or groundcover. Good for texture change.
PROBLEMS:	Snails and slugs sometimes. Usually not a big problem.
NOTES:	Also called Monkey Grass and Lilyturf. Variegated form exists called 'Silvery Sunproof.' My favorites are the green forms, 'Big Blue' and 'Majestic.' The giant form, *L. gigantea*, is also good. Native to China and Japan.

MANDEVILLA

Mandevilla x 'Alice du Pont'
man-da-VEE-yah

Tropical · Sun
Vine
Spacing 3'-7'

HABIT:	Fast, climbing vine with large oval leaves and pink trumpet-like flowers that bloom from early summer till the first hard freeze. Needs wire or structure to get started. Also a lovely white flowering variety.
CULTURE:	Treat this tropical vine as an annual — when it freezes, throw away. Likes well prepared soil, moisture and regular fertilization.
USES:	Climbing vine for summer color. Good in pots set by post or arbor.
PROBLEMS:	Few if any. Red spider if in stress.
NOTES:	Tough and dramatic annual color. I highly recommend. Native to Central and South America.

MONEYWORT

Lysimachia nummularia
liz-se-MACH-ee-ah num-mew-LARR-ee-ah

Evergreen · Shade/Part Shade
Ht. 3" Groundcover
Spacing 9"-12"

HABIT:	Very low growing, soft round leaves, spreads by runners. Roots easily where stem touches ground.
CULTURE:	Grows best in shade or part shade in moist, well prepared beds.
USES:	Groundcover for small shady places.
PROBLEMS:	Starts easily from broken pieces in areas where it may not be wanted.
NOTES:	Also called Creeping Jennie. Native to Europe.

OPHIOPOGON
Ophiopogon japonicum
oh-fee-oh-POE-gon ja-PON-eh-cum

Evergreen · Shade/Part Shade
Ht. 8"-10" Groundcover
Spacing 9"

HABIT: Low growing, grass-like groundcover. Grows in clumps but spreads by rhizomes to form solid mass.
CULTURE: Best in shade or partial shade but will grow in sun. Needs even moisture and regular fertilization. Mow down once per year in late winter just before the new growth breaks.
USES: Low groundcover for small to medium size areas.
PROBLEMS: Nematodes, rabbits.
NOTES: Also called Mondo Grass or Monkey Grass. A dwarf form, *O. japonicum* 'nana,' is very compact, dark green and slow growing. It should be planted at least 6" on center. A black form exists that is expensive and extremely slow growing. Native to Japan and Korea.

PACHYSANDRA
Pachysandra terminalis
pack-eh-SAND-drah term-eh-NAH-lus

Evergreen · Shade
Ht. 6"-8" Groundcover
Spacing 9"-12"

HABIT: Low growing groundcover, spreads by underground stems (rhizomes). Does best in higher organic soils in deep shade.
CULTURE: Plant in well prepared, shaded area. Needs lots of organic material, good drainage, ample water and fertilizer.
USES: Groundcover for small areas in heavy shade, interesting foliage texture.
PROBLEMS: Summer heat. Also doesn't like our alkaline soils. Leaf blight, scale, nematodes.
NOTES: Native to Japan. Also called Japanese Spurge.

PASSION VINE
Passiflora incarnata
pass-sih-FLO-ruh in-kar-NAY-tuh

Perennial · Sun
Vine
Spacing 3'-6'

HABIT: Large, deeply cut leaves, climbs quickly by tendrils. Blooms almost all summer with spectacular purple and white flowers.
CULTURE: Easy, any soil, drought tolerant. Dies to the ground each winter but returns in spring.
USES: Summer climbing vine, flower display.
PROBLEMS: None.
NOTES: Native from east Texas to Florida. The introduced varieties also have dramatic flowers but most are not winter hearty.

POTENTILLA
Potentilla verna
poe-ten-TEA-ah VER-na

(not & grown)
buck yard next
to patio (?)

Evergreen · Sun/Shade
Ht. 2"-6" Groundcover
Spacing 6"-9"

HABIT: Light textured, low growing groundcover. Resembles tiny strawberry plants. Small yellow flowers in summer.
CULTURE: Partial shade is best, any soil, but responds to well prepared and well drained beds. Moderate water and fertilizer needs.
USES: Groundcover for small to medium size areas.
PROBLEMS: Red spider, rust.
NOTES: Plant gets a little weedy. Avoid using in large areas. Native to Europe.

ROSE, LADY BANK'S

Rosa banksia
ROW-sa BANK-see-ah

Semi-evergreen · Sun
Vine
Spacing 4'-8'

HABIT: Massive, free-flowing, bushy vine. Shoots grow up and arch over. Small yellow or white flowers.
CULTURE: Likes even moisture but is fairly drought tolerant. Tough, grows in any soil; well prepared soil is better. Low maintenance other than pruning to control aggressive growth.
USES: Vining rose for walls, fences, overhead-structures.
PROBLEMS: Fast growing, regular pruning.
NOTES: This plant needs plenty of room — not good for small garden spaces. Native to China. 'Alba Plena' is the white flowering cultivar.

SEDUM

Sedum spp.
SEE-dum

Evergreen · Sun/Part Shade
Ht. 2"-6" Groundcover
Spacing 6"-9"

HABIT: Finely textured, succulent groundcover. Easily damaged by foot traffic or pets when the succulent leaves and stems are crushed.
CULTURE: Easy, any soil, prefers well prepared and drained beds. Best exposure is partial shade.
USES: Groundcover for small areas, Oriental gardens, rock gardens, stone walls and small accent areas.
PROBLEMS: Damage from foot traffic.
NOTES: Native to Europe and Asia. *Sedum* 'Autumn Joy' is a tall growing perennial with dramatic flowers that are white as they start developing in the summer and end up red in the fall. S. 'Ruby Glow' is lower growing and blooms all summer.

ST. AUGUSTINEGRASS

Stenotaphrum secundatum
sten-no TAY-frum seh-coon-DAY-tum

Warm season · Sun/Shade
Mowing Ht. 2"
Solid sod

HABIT: Wide bladed grass, spreads by stolons, most shade tolerant of our warm season grasses. 'Raleigh' is a hybrid resistant to St. Augustine decline (SAD), and is more cold hearty than hybrids 'Seville' and 'Floratam'.
CULTURE: Any well drained soil that is fairly fertile. Not as tough as Bermudagrass.
USES: Lawn grass, shade.
PROBLEMS: Chinch bugs, grub worms, diseases.
NOTES: Native to Africa and the Gulf Coast.

STRAWBERRY, FALSE

Duchesnea indica
doo-CHEZ-ne-ah IN-dee-cah

Evergreen · Sun/Part Shade
Ht. 3"-6" Groundcover
Spacing 9"-12"

HABIT: Low growing groundcover that spreads by runners and by seeds. Looks like the regular strawberry but the fruit doesn't develop. It's red but much smaller and tastes like cardboard.
CULTURE: Easy, any soil, fairly drought tolerant.
USES: Groundcover for unrefined gardens.
PROBLEMS: Spreads badly — very invasive.
NOTES: I learned the hard way that this stuff takes over the entire garden by popping up everywhere. Native to USA and South America.

THYME, CREEPING

Thymus spp.
TIME-us

Perennial - Sun
Ht. 1"-18" Groundcover
Spacing 6"-12"

HABIT:	Low growing and spreading herb with flowers of white, pink and lavender. Three groups: upright sub shrubs 12"-18", creeping herbs 3"-6" and flat creepers 1"-2" tall. The larger plants are the culinary forms.
CULTURE:	Well drained and prepared beds. Protection from the strong afternoon sun is ideal. Moderate fertilizer and water needs.
USES:	Groundcover, perennial gardens, containers and baskets, fragrance.
PROBLEMS:	Extreme weather fluctuations.
NOTES:	The Creeping Thymes cross pollinate freely, causing a mix of flower color, but that is nice. Coconut, Lemon, Caraway and Mother of Thyme are good choices.

TRUMPET VINE (Native)

Campsis radicans
KAMP-sis RAD-ee-kans

Deciduous - Sun/Part Shade
Vine
Spacing 5'-8'

HABIT:	Large sprawling vine with showy orange and red trumpet like flowers that bloom all summer. Climbs by aerial roots. Bare in winter.
CULTURE:	Easy to grow in any soil, drought tolerant. Prune back to the main trunk after leaves fall in the spring.
USES:	Climby vine for fence, arbor, screens or poles. Summer flower color.
PROBLEMS:	Native plant spreads, causing a maintenance problem.
NOTES:	Native to the east coast, Florida and Texas. 'Madame Galen' introduced by French nurseries doesn't spread as much as the native plant. *C. radicans* 'Flava' has pure yellow flowers. *C.* x 'Crimson Trumpet' is a pure red.

VINCA

Vinca major (minor)
VIN-cah

Evergreen - Shade/Part Shade
Ht. 6"-18" Groundcover
Spacing 12"

HABIT:	Coarse groundcover for large areas in shade. Spreads quickly and has blue flowers in late spring.
CULTURE:	Plant in any soil in shade. Relatively drought tolerant once established.
USES:	Good plant for a naturally wooded area.
PROBLEMS:	Leaf rollers, cutworms.
NOTES:	Native to Europe and Asia. Not very good to use on residential property where closely inspected. *V. major* is the large leafed, more commonly used variety. *V. minor* has smaller, shinier leaves, is more refined in appearance and can tolerate more sun.

VIRGINIA CREEPER (Native)

Parthenocissus quinquefolia
par-thuh-no-SIS-us kwin-kuh-FOLE-ee-uh

Deciduous - Sun/Shade
Vine
Spacing 3'-8'

HABIT:	Vigorous climbing vine. Looser growth and larger leaves than Boston Ivy. Red foliage in fall. Climbs to great heights.
CULTURE:	Needs pruning to keep under control. Any soil in sun or shade. Responds well to well prepared beds and moderate water and fertilizer.
USES:	Interesting texture and good fall color. Good for arbor, fence or large building.
PROBLEMS:	None serious.
NOTES:	Often confused with Poison Ivy. This plant has five leaflets instead of Poison Ivy's three. Native to Texas and eastern USA.

WINTERCREEPER, PURPLE

Euonymus fortunei 'Coloratus'
you-ON-eh-mus for-TUNE-ee-eye call-oh-RAY-tus

Evergreen · Sun/Shade
8"-12" Groundcover
Spacing 12"

HABIT: Evergreen groundcover, spreads by runners; reddish fall color that lasts through winter. Sun or partial shade is best exposure. Moderate water and fertilization. Establishes fast if planted properly with mulch applied after planting.
CULTURE: Well drained and prepared beds. Moderate water and fertilization requirements.
USES: Groundcover for large areas.
PROBLEMS: Scale occasionally.
NOTES: Avoid *Euonymus radicans* and other larger leafed varieties. Native to China.

WISTERIA, CHINESE

Wisteria sinensis
wiss-TER-ee-ah sigh-NEN-sis

Deciduous · Sun/Part Shade
Vine
Spacing 8'-10'

HABIT: Fast growing, twining vine that can grow to great heights. Purple spring flowers. 'Alba' has white flowers. Japanese Wisteria *(W. floribunda)* has longer flowers which don't open until the foliage is on the plant.
CULTURE: Easy, any soil.
USES: Climbing vine for arbor, fence or wall. Spring flowers.
PROBLEMS: Can take over if not pruned to keep in shape. Grasshoppers.
NOTES: Most Wisteria are native to China.

WISTERIA, EVERGREEN

Millettia reticulata
mill-LEE-she-ah re-ti-cue-LA-tah

Evergreen · Sun/Part Shade
Vine
Spacing 5'-8'

HABIT: Climbing vine having lighter and more refined growth and texture than regular Wisteria. Sparse purple orchid-like flowers in summer.
CULTURE: Loose, well drained soil. Moderate water and fertilizer.
USES: Evergreen climbing vine, fences, arbors, etc.
PROBLEMS: Possible freeze damage.
NOTES: New to the scene. Use with caution for awhile. I think it will be a winner. Native to China.

ZOYSIAGRASS

Zoysia japonica 'Meyeri'
ZOY-sha jap-PON-eh-kah

Warm season · Sun/Part Shade
Mowing Ht. 2"
Solid sod

HABIT: Thick, succulent looking grass. Very slow to spread.
CULTURE: Plant solid sod only, too slow growing for any other planting techniques.
USES: Lawn grass, small areas, Oriental gardens.
PROBLEMS: Slow — but that gives it its maintenance advantages. Thatch build up.
NOTES: Avoid using in high traffic areas. 'Meyer' is wider leafed and better than 'Emerald' which is a narrow leaf. Zoysia can be mowed less often than Bermuda and St. Augustine and it requires far less edging. Native to Japan.

FLOWERS:
ANNUALS, PERENNIALS
AND BULBS

EASY REFERENCE FOR FLOWERS

FALL COLOR

Aster
Calendua
Candletree
Chrysanthemum
Marigold
Salvia, Regla
Sedum, Autumn Joy

WINTER COLOR

Calendua
Dianthus
Kale
Lentenrose
Pansy
Snapdragon

SPRING COLOR

Alyssum	Iris
Anemone	Lamb's Ear
Aster, Stoke's	Mexican Blanket
Bluebonnet	Mexican Hat
Butterfly Iris	Oxalis
Candytuft	Peony
Coralbell	Petunia
Coreopsis	Phlox
Cornflower	Poppy
Daffodil	Rose
Daisy	Snapdragon
Daylilly	Thrift
Dianthus	Tulip
Foxglove	Wallflower
Geranium	Yarrow
Horsemint	

SUMMER COLOR (SUN)

Ageratum	Jacobina
Alyssum	Lantana
Aster, Frikarti	Lisianthus
	Lythrum
Aster, Stokes	Marigold
Begonia	Nierembergia
Candletree	Oxalis
Canna	Penta
Chenille Plant	Periwinkle
Copperleaf	Phlox
Coreopsis	Plumbago
Cosmos	Portulaca
Dahlia	Purple Coneflower
Daisy	Rose
	Rosemary
Dusty Miller	Salvia
Gayfeather	Spider Lilies
Gazania	Turk's Cap
Hibiscus	Verbena
Hollyhocks	Wallflower
	Zinnia

SUMMER COLOR (SHADE)

Astilbe	Geranium
Begonia	Impatiens
Caladium	Lobelia
Coleus	Rock Rose
Columbine	Plumeria
Crocosmia	

ANNUALS AND PERENNIALS

Ageratum (*A. houstonianum*) — Blue or white flowering annual, sun or part shade, height to 15", small round fluffy flowers in summer.

Amaranth, Globe (*Gomphrena globosa*) — Buddy Plant, is small growing annual with 1" round, clover-like flowers of almost any color. Sun.

Astilbe (*Astilbe* spp.) — Early summer blooming perennial spire-like flowers of white, pink or red. Likes moist soil and partial shade. Some varieties are more drought tolerant than others.

Bouncing Bet (*Saponaria officinalis*) — Evergreen perennial, fragrant phlox-like pink flowers all summer.

Butterfly Weed (*Asclepias tuberosa*) — Sun perennial, loves the heat, does best in deep, well prepared soil. Also called Pleurisy Root. Orange flowers all summer. Full sun.

Calendula (*Calendula officinalis*) — Also called English Marigold. Cool season annual best used in full sun. Not fussy about soil or culture. Mostly yellows and oranges.

Chenille Plant (*Acalypha hispida*) — Annual foliage and flower plant, kin to copperleaf but has long red fuzzy flowers and less colorful foliage. Very tender to cold weather.

Coralbell (*Hencherella* spp.) — Showy perennial that blooms in sun or shade from spring till fall.

Cornflower (*Centaurea cyanus*) — Also called Bachelor's Button. Annual wildflower with blue, white and pink flowers in late spring.

Crocosmia (*C. pottsii*) — Perennial that grows and spreads readily in full sun to fairly heavy shade. Red-orange flowers in early summer.

Evolvulus — Annual with small blue flowers and gray sage-like foliage. Blooms all summer long. Good annual for hanging baskets also.

Foxglove (*Digitalis* spp.) — Annual, best in partial shade. White, yellow, pink and red flowers along a vertical stalk in spring or early summer. Entire plant it poisonous.

Heather, Mexican (*Hyssopifolia* spp.) — False heather, annual with small purple flowers all summer on lacy foliage.

Hollyhocks (*Althea rosea*) — Biennial or perennial herbs with clusters of flowers along tall shoots. Many colors available. Sun.

Horsemint (*Monarda citridora*) — Also called Lemonmint, a wildflower blooming in late spring with aromatic rosy-pink to purple flowers. Full sun.

Hummingbird Bush (*Anisacanthus wrightii*) — Small orange flowered perennial. Tough, spreads easily, attracts hummingbirds.

Ice Plant (*Mesembryanthemum crystallimum*) — Tender succulent used here as an annual. Good in rock walls or any well drained area. Full sun.

Iris, Butterfly (*Moraea bicolor*) — Iris-like plant that blooms with small yellow flowers in spring. Full sun.

Jacobinia or Brazilian Plume Flower (*Jacobinia carnea*) — Also called Rat Plant, tropical shrub used as summer annual. Purple, pink or white blossoms. Best in sunny moist spot. Can be overwintered easily indoors and reused outside the following spring.

Kale, Flowering (*Brassica oleracea acephala*) — Cabbage relative with rosy or whitish foliage color in the winter months. Plant in fall, can freeze in severe winter, is edible. Flowering cabbage is also good. Sun.

Lamb's Ear (*Stachys byzintina*) — Perennial with soft gray fuzzy leaves and lavender flower spikes in late spring. Sun.

Lentenrose (*Helleborus orientalis*) — Perennial that blooms winter to early spring. White or pink flowers. The roots are extremely poisonous. Sun or part shade.

Spider Lily White variety (*Hymenocallis liriosme*) — is a perennial bulb that likes wet soil and blooms in spring. Red spider lily (*Lycoris radiata*) has red flowers in mid to late summer. Sun to part shade.

Lobelia (*Lobelia* spp.) — Blue, purple or red flowering annual. Best here if protected from afternoon sun.

Mexican Blanket (*Gaillardia* spp.) — Multi-colored spring wildflower: mostly reds, yellows and oranges. Full sun.

Mexican Hat (*Ratibida columnaris*) — Native wildflower that blooms late spring to early summer. Flowers have droopy petals on upright stems — thus the name. Yellow and reddish brown colors primarily. Full sun.

Obedient Plant (*Physostegia* spp.) — Is a carefree perennial, spring or fall bloom. Also called Lionheart. Several colors.

Peony (*Paeonia* spp.) — Bushy perennial, flowers of red, pink, white in spring or early summer. Needs highly organic soil. Sun.

Phlox (*Phlox* spp.) — Several varieties and colors, spring and summer color, full sun or part shade. Summer or Garden Phlox is the most common. *Phlox paniculata* 'Mt. Fugi' is a lovely white selection.

Plumeria (*Plumeria* spp.) — Gorgeous tropical with long pointed leaves and flowers all summer. Must be protected in winter. Good in pots. Sun or part shade.

Red Hot Poker (*Kniphofia* spp.), syn. *Tritoma* — Grassy-leafed perennial with brilliant coral-red flower clusters which become orange and yellow with age.

Rock Rose (*Pavonia lasiopetala*) — Shrubby perennial with small pink flowers all summer. Native to Texas and Mexico, drought tolerant and likes our soil. Sun or part shade.

Shrimp Plant (*Beloperone guttata*) — Terra cotta to lemon yellow bracts with small white flowers that arch to the side. Full sun. Close kin is Lollipop Plant (*Pachystachys lutea*), which has bright yellow bracts which are vertical. Needs partial shade. Both are used as annuals here.

Turk's Cap (*Malvaviscus drummondii*) — Red flowering perennial, 3'-5' height, blooms all summer. Good for attracting hummingbirds. Flowers resemble a fez — thus the name. Full sun.

Wallflower (*Cheiranthus* spp.) — Yellow, red, orange or purple flowers. Sun or shade. For fall and cool weather flowers.

ALYSSUM
Alyssum spp.
ah-LIS-um

Annual - Sun
Ht. 3"-4" Spread 9"-12"
Spacing 6"

HABIT:	Low growing, small delicate flowers of white and lavender which bloom in summer.
CULTURE:	Requires little care but is damaged easily by foot traffic and pets. Any soil, relatively drought tolerant.
USES:	Rock gardens, pockets in stonewalls, small accent areas of annual color.
PROBLEMS:	Few if any.
NOTES:	Is native to Turkey.

ANEMONE
Anemone spp.
ah-NEM-oh-nee

Annual - Sun
Ht. 6"-15", Spread 6"-12"
Spacing 6"-9"

HABIT:	Lacy foliage and colorful poppy-like flowers in spring. All colors but yellow. Actually a tuberous root, but performs like an annual.
CULTURE:	Plant in full sun or partial shade with the claws pointed down late winter (no cold hours required). Must be replanted each year here.
USES:	Multi-colored spring flowers.
PROBLEMS:	Aphids, cutworms.
NOTES:	Use a knife or clippers to pick Anemones because pulling may tear the crown of the tuber. *Ranunculus repens* is a very similar plant but taller. Japanese Anemone *(A. japonica)* is a lovely perennial that blooms primarily in the fall.

ASTER
Aster frikarti
AS-ter fri-CAR-tie

Perennial - Sun
Ht. 1'-3', Spread 2'-4'
Spacing 12"-18"

HABIT:	Daisy-like perennial that blooms summer through fall. Light blue flowers.
CULTURE:	Plant in well prepared and drained beds. Moderate water and fertilization requirements. Divide established plants in spring every 3-4 years.
USES:	Fall color, border. Cutting gardens. Considered to be one of the best perennial flowers in the world.
PROBLEMS:	Cutworms, powdery mildew. Can be over watered easily.
NOTES:	Plant in fall or early spring. The Hardy Blue Aster is the common fall blooming variety. Many other varieties and colors available but *frikarti* is the most showy and blooms the longest. Others mainly bloom in the fall. Two good cultivars of *frikarti* are 'Wonder of Staffa' and 'Moench'.

ASTER, STOKES
Stokesia laevis
STOKES-ee-ah LAY-vis

Perennial - Sun/Part Shade
Ht. 2' Spread 2'-3'
Spacing 1"-18"

HABIT:	Long narrow leaves, daisy-like flowers bloom mid summer through fall.
CULTURE:	Likes loose, moist soil and light fertilization. Tolerant of heat and a fair amount of neglect. Easy to grow.
USES:	Perennial garden, summer flowers.
PROBLEMS:	Few if any.
NOTES:	Larger, more intricate flower than the real aster. It is a worldwide plant.

BEGONIA

Begonia spp.
beh-GON-ee-ah

Annual - Sun/Shade
Ht. 6"-15" Spread 12"-18"
Spacing 9"-12"

HABIT: Erect or trailing; soft shiny foliage that is sometimes red. Blooms throughout the summer.
CULTURE: Needs loose, well prepared beds, lots of organic material and good positive drainage. Some varieties need sun, others shade.
USES: Summer color, hanging baskets, pots.
PROBLEMS: Slugs, cutworms.
NOTES: Plants grown in pots can be moved indoors and saved through winter. Plant after the last freeze. Native to Brazil.

BLUEBONNETT (Native)

Lupinus texensis
loo-PEEN-us tex-IN-sis

Annual - Sun
Ht. 9"-12" Spread 12"-15"
Seeds @ 1 lb/1000 s.f.

HABIT: Upright to sprawling spring wildflower. Germinates from seed in fall, leaves and stems hairy. Flowers have wonderful fragrance.
CULTURE: Sometimes hard to get going but once established is reliable each year.
USES: Wildflower.
PROBLEMS: Hard seed to germinate.
NOTES: Do not fertilize wildflowers. Native to Texas. Nurseries are now selling 2¼" pots for planting small garden areas in the spring.

CALADIUM

Caladium x *hortulanum*
ca-LAY-dee-um hor-too-LAN-um

Annual - Shade/Partial Shade
Ht. 2' Spread 12"-18"
Spacing 8"-12"

HABIT: Brightly colored leaves on tall stems from tubers. White varieties seem to be more sun tolerant.
CULTURE: Plant tubers in well prepared beds after the soil temperaters have warmed in the later spring (April 15-30). Dies at frost. Not worth trying to save the tubers through the winter. Keep the flowers cut off. Mix bone meal into beds before planting (1 tablespoon per tuber).
USES: Color in groundcover areas, containers.
PROBLEMS: Wind damage.
NOTES: The whites are my favorites, such as 'Candidum' (shown in photo), 'Arron,' 'White Wing' and 'Jackie Suthers.' Mother plants are native to the riverbanks of the Amazon.

CANDLETREE

Cassia alata
CASS-ee-ah ah-LAY-tah

Annual - Sun
Ht. 6'-8' Spread 6'-8'
Spacing 3'-4'

HABIT: Open spreading growth in summer. Yellow flowers in spiked clusters. Large compound leaves. Gets large in one season.
CULTURE: Needs sun, loose organic soil and moderate water and fertilization. Prune back after flowering.
USES: Dramatic accent plant, late summer color, background and annual color for large open areas.
NOTES: Parks departments use together with Cannas for a carefree colorful show. Native to the tropics.

CANDYTUFT

Iberis sempervirens
eye-BER-is sem-per-VIE-rens

Perennial - Sun/Part Shade
Ht. 8"-12" Spread 12'-15'
Spacing 9"-12"

HABIT:	Low, compact, neat perennial that produces pure white flowers that bloom in spring. Will usually return year after year.
CULTURE:	Plant in sun or partial shade in well prepared soil that drains easily. Moderate water and fertilizer requirements.
USES:	Small gardens, rock walls, small containers.
PROBLEMS:	Few if any.
NOTES:	Also called Evergreen or Perennial Candytuft.

CANNA

Canna generalis
CAN-ah jen-er-ALL-is

Perennial - Sun
Ht. 2'-6' Spread 3'-6'
Spacing 18"-24"

HABIT:	Coarse perennial that spreads from underground stems. Large leaves and flowers. Most popular is dwarf red. Dies to ground at frost, returns the next spring.
CULTURE:	Full sun, loose soil, plenty of water and healthy amounts of fertilizer for good blooms.
USES:	Use as a background flower or in large open areas.
PROBLEMS:	Wind damage, coarseness.
NOTES:	Easy to grow but too coarse for most residential gardens. Native to the tropics. The red foliage selections tend to have smaller flowers but are better looking plants.

CHRYSANTHEMUM (MUM)

Chrysanthemum spp.
kris-AN-tha-mum

Perennial - Sun
Ht. 12"-36" Spread 18"-36"
Spacing 12"-18"

HABIT:	Fall blooming perennials, lots of colors and combinations. Attractive foliage that looks good most of the year. Some bloom in spring and fall.
CULTURE:	Loose soil, good drainage, ample water and regular fertilization. For best blooms, pinch new growth out until August 1st. Stop fertilization when the buds show color. Avoid light at night for it retards blooms.
USES:	Perennial gardens, border, pots, cutting gardens.
PROBLEMS:	Aphids.
NOTES:	There are 13 different categories established by National Chrysanthemum Society: Spoon, Reflexing Incurve, Semi-double, Decorative, Anemone, Spider, Single, Reflex, Pompom, Thistle, Laciniated, Quile and Incurve. They are all beautiful. Native to Europe, Asia and South Africa.

COLEUS

Coleus blumei
COLE-ee-uh BLOOM-ee-eye

Annual - Shade
Ht. 18"-24" Spread 18"-24"
Spacing 12"-18"

HABIT:	Colorful leaves of red, yellow, orange, green and all combinations. Dies at frost, very tender.
CULTURE:	Need shade, drainage, moisture and protection from wind. Keep flowers pinched off.
USES:	Summer color, border or mass. Containers or hanging baskets.
PROBLEMS:	Slugs, snails, mealybugs and aphids.
NOTES:	Roots easily in water and can be grown indoors. Native to the tropics.

COLUMBINE (Native)

Aquilegia spp.
ah-kwi-LEE-ji-ah

good y wildflwa bed

Perennial - Shade/Part Shade
Ht. 12"-18" Spread 12"-18"
Spacing 12"

HABIT:	Delicate, woodsy-type flowers that bloom on long stems from lacy foliage. Dies to ground at frost, returns the following spring.
CULTURE:	Loose, well drained soil. Light water and fertilizer requirements.
USES:	Color in shady area.
PROBLEMS:	Few if any.
NOTES:	*A. canadensis* is the red and yellow flowered native and is very carefree. *A. longissima* is the pure yellow native that gets 24"-3' tall.

CONEFLOWER, PURPLE (Native)

Echinacea angustifolia
ek-uh-NAY-see-uh an-gus-ti-FOAL-ee-ah

Perennial - Sun
Ht. 2'-3' Spread 3'-4'
Spacing 1'-2'

HABIT:	Brightly flowered perennial that blooms early to mid summer. Flowers are dark pink with yellow centers.
CULTURE:	Carefree and drought tolerant.
USES:	Perennial beds, natural areas and most anywhere — it's a great plant.
PROBLEMS:	Few if any.
NOTES:	*E. purpurea* is a lower blooming variety with larger flowers. *E.* 'White Swan' is a white flowering cultivar.

COPPERLEAF

Acalypha wilkesiana
ah-ca-LEE-fa wilk-see-AN-ah

Annual - Sun
Ht. 24"-36" Spread 24"-36"
Spacing 18"

HABIT:	Fast growing tropical shrub that works like an annual for us. Flowers are insignificant. Colorful foliage all summer. Dies at frost.
CULTURE:	Best in full sun, prepared beds, good drainage and ample water and fertilizer.
USES:	Background for other bedding plants.
PROBLEMS:	Extensive root system often competes with other bedding plants.
NOTES:	Also called Copper Plant. Native to the Pacific Islands.

COREOPSIS (Native)

Coreopsis spp.
ko-ree-OP-sis

Perennial - Sun
Ht. 12"-24" Spread 24"
Spacing 12"-24"

HABIT:	Perennial that looks good most of the year and great while in bloom May to August. Will reseed and spread — which is OK. Primarily yellow flowers.
CULTURE:	Easy in any soil, sun to light shade, low water and food needs. Can be planted from seed.
USES:	Summer color, perennial beds, cut flowers.
PROBLEMS:	None.
NOTES:	*C. lanceolata* is a pure yellow native. Several hybrids such as 'Sun Ray' and 'Baby Sun' are on the market which are excellent. *C. tinctoria* is an annual with a red center. There are many other choices and most all of them are good.

COSMOS

Cosmos parviflorus
KOS-mos par-vi-FLOR-us

Annual - Sun
Ht. 12"-18" Spread 18"-24"
Spacing 12"

HABIT:	Lacy foliage and flowers on long stems. Multi-colored flowers in summer. White is best.
CULTURE:	Any soil, drought tolerant. Can be easily grown from seed. Plant late spring or early summer.
USES:	Summer flowers.
PROBLEMS:	Few if any. Fungus if planted too early in the season.
NOTES:	Plant from seed directly in beds after last frost and beyond. Native to Mexico.

DAFFODIL

Narcissus spp.
narr-SIS-us

Perennial - Sun
Ht 9"-18" Spread 12"-18"
Spacing 6"-12"

HABIT:	Lovely bell shaped flowers in early spring. Colors are white, yellow, orange and combinations. Foliage of vertical blades from the ground.
CULTURE:	Plant bulbs in loose organic beds with good drainage. Add 1 tablespoon bone meal per bulb and work into the soil before planting. Foliage must be left to turn brown on the plant before removing to form the bulbs for next year.
USES:	Spring flowers, naturalized area, cutting garden.
PROBLEMS:	Snails, slugs.
NOTES:	Flowers last about two weeks, usually less. Don't invest a lot of money in Daffodils. The smaller white Narcissus has same characteristics. Also called Jonquil.

DAHLIA

Dahlia spp.
DAL-ee-ah

Perennial - Sun
Ht. 2'-6' Spread 2'-4'
Spacing 12"-24"

HABIT:	Colorful flowers that bloom from spring to fall. Does not bloom well in the hotter parts of the summer. Dwarf varieties are the best here.
CULTURE:	Needs sun, rich porous soil and heavy amounts of fertilizer. Plant in February or March. Cultivate around plants until blooms form, then mulch heavily.
USES:	Summer flowers, background plant for perennial beds, cut flowers.
PROBLEMS:	Heat, red spider mites.
NOTES:	Dahlia is the national flower of Mexico.

DIANTHUS

Dianthus spp.
dye-AN-thus

Perennials - Sun
Ht. 8'-12' Spread 12'-18'
Spacing 9'-12'

HABIT:	Delicate looking cool weather flowers that come in a variety of colors ranging from reds and purples to pinks and whites. Some are annual, others perennial. Some varieties will bloom all winter if weather is not severe.
CULTURE:	Prepared and well drained beds in full sun. Moderate water and fertilizer.
USES:	Cool season color.
PROBLEMS:	None serious.
NOTES:	Plant in the fall or late winter. A good perennial variety is *D. allwoodii*. Carnations, Pinks and Sweet Williams are all variations of this genus.

DAISY, BLACKFOOT (Native)

Melampodium cinereum
mel-lam-PODE-ee-um sin-ear-RE-um

Perennial - Sun/Part Shade
Ht. 12" Spread 12"-15"
Spacing 9"-12"

HABIT:	Low growing, compact daisy. White blossoms all growing season long. Dies to the ground in winter. Returns faithfully each year.
CULTURE:	Easy in any soil.
USES:	Perennial garden; border; white spring, summer, fall flowers.
PROBLEMS:	None.
NOTES:	Easy to transplant or plant any time of the year. This is one of my favorites. A taller growing yellow variety also exists and is quite good. It is an annual.

DAISY, GLORIOSA (Native)

Rudbeckia birta
rude-BECK-ee-ah HIR-ta

Perennial - Sun
Ht. 18"-3' Spread 18"-24"
Spacing 12"-18"

HABIT:	Fuzzy foliage and yellow flowers with dark brown centers that bloom June into August.
CULTURE:	Grows OK in dry soil but responds favorably to moist well prepared beds. Needs good drainage.
USES:	Summer flowers, low water areas.
PROBLEMS:	None.
NOTES:	Also called Cone Flower and Black-Eyed Susan. Native to Texas. *Rudbeckia* 'Goldstrum' is an improved variety. Can be planted from seed or pots.

DAISY, OXEYE (Native)

Chrysanthemum leucanthemum
kruh-SAN-thuh-mum loo-KAN-thuh-mum

Perennial - Sun
Ht. 12"-36" Spread 18"-36"
Spacing 12"-18"

HABIT:	Large showy flowers that are great for cutting from early June to August. Returns very well each year.
CULTURE:	Easy, any well drained soil. Low water and fertilizer requirement. Established plants should be divided every few years.
USES:	Summer flowers, perennial gardens.
PROBLEMS:	None serious.
NOTES:	Cut flowers have a bad odor. This plant is similar to Shasta Daisy but tougher and more drought tolerant. Dwarf Shasta Daisy is also a good choice and 'Silver Princess' is a particularly good one. Tahoka Daisy is a Texas native that blooms all summer with blue flowers. Lazy Daisy is a low growing annual.

DAYLILLY

Hemerocallis spp.
him-er-oh-CALL-us

Perennial - Sun/Part Shade
Ht. 8"-36" Spread 24"-36"
Spacing 18"-24"

HABIT:	Foliage-like large leafed grass. Many colors, shapes of blooms and height of plants available. Blooms from late May till September. Each bloom lasts only one day but others follow. Blooms range in size from 2"-8" across.
CULTURE:	Easy, any well prepared and drained soil. Average water and heavy fertilizer needs. Divide in October or November every few years. Plant from containers year round.
USES:	Summer flowers, background or accent plant, cut flowers.
PROBLEMS:	Few serious.
NOTES:	Called Poor Man's Orchid. Plant divisions in the fall. Container plants can actually be planted any time of the year. Native to Europe, China and Japan. Daylillies are a gourmet vegetable.

DUSTY MILLER

Centaurea cineraria
sin-TAU-ree-ah sin-er-RARE-ee-ah

Perennial - Sun
Ht. 18"-24" Spread 18"-24"
Spacing 12"

HABIT:	Distinctive plant with fuzzy, silver-gray foliage and yellow flowers in early summer.
CULTURE:	Plant in full sun, any well drained soil, moderate water and fertilizer.
USES:	Color contrast, drought tolerant gardens, stone walls, pots.
PROBLEMS:	Few if any.
NOTES:	Plant from containers anytime. Native to southern Europe.

GAYFEATHER (Native)

Liatris spp.
lee-AT-tris

Perennial - Sun
Ht. 1'-2' Spread 1'-2'
Spacing 1'-2'

HABIT:	Tufts of narrow stems topped by narrow plumes of fluffy purple flowers.
CULTURE:	Tough, drought tolerant wildflowers that respond fairly well to maintained gardens. Cut to the ground in winter. Can be planted from pots or seed.
USES:	Perennial gardens, borders, summer flowers.
PROBLEMS:	Too much water.
NOTES	Makes wonderful cut flower because the purple color lasts indefinitely in a dry arrangement. Several good varieties exist. Native to Texas and Oklahoma.

GAZANIA

Gazania hybrids
ga-ZANE-ee-ah

Perennial - Sun
Ht 6"-12" Spread 12"-18"
Spacing 9"-12"

HABIT:	Clump-forming summer flower. Mostly yellows and oranges.
CULTURE:	Plant in full sun, any soil with good drainage. Drought tolerant and low fertilization requirements.
USES:	Summer color, drought tolerant gardens.
PROBLEMS:	None.
NOTES:	Native to South Africa. Plant from containers in spring.

GERANIUM

Pelargonium hortorum
pell-ar-GONE-ee-um hor-TORE-um

Annual - Sun/Part Shade
Ht. 18"-24" Spread 18"-24"
Spacing 12"

HABIT:	Upright or trailing; clusters of red, orange, pink or white flowers.
CULTURE:	Sun or part shade, well prepared beds with good drainage. Cool weather is its favorite time of the year. Plant in late winter from containers.
USES:	Annual gardens, pots, hanging baskets.
PROBLEMS:	Cutworms, caterpillars, summer heat.
NOTES:	A little cold weather is good for them. Native to South Africa. *Geranium* spp. is the true Geranium. It is a smaller plant but perennial. Scented Geraniums bloom only once a year and are grown mostly for their wonderfully varied fragrances.

HIBISCUS

Hibiscus moscheutos
hi-BIS-cus ma-SHU-tos

Perennial · Sun/Part Shade
Ht. 5'-6' Spread 3'-6'
Spacing 2'-3'

HABIT:	Upright, thick succulent stems. Many colors and characteristics available. Blooms all summer.
CULTURE:	Easy; any well drained soil, moderate water and fertilizer requirements. Native to the southern USA.
USES:	Summer flower color, specimen, pots.
PROBLEMS:	Few if any.
NOTES:	There are many other Hibiscus that are wonderful plants. The tropicals which act as annuals here are the most colorful but the hearty perennials Rose-Mallow *(H. moscheutos)* are beautiful and will usually overwinter. Another wonderful perennial is Texas Star *(H. coccineus)*. 'Frisbee,' 'Southern Bell,' 'Confederate' and 'Marsh' are excellent perennial cultivars.

HYACINTH

Hyacinth spp.
HI-ah-sinth

Perennial · Sun
Ht. 3"-12" Spread 3"-12"
Spacing 6"-9"

HABIT:	Vertical foliage in spring followed by dramatic flower spike of most any color. Extremely fragrant.
CULTURE:	Well prepared, well drained soil; moderate water and fertilizer requirements. Add bone meal to soil when planting.
USES:	Spring color, fragrance.
PROBLEMS:	Expensive for the show.
NOTES:	Plant bulbs in December for early spring flowers. Plants will return but will be quite weak. Better to plant new ones again. *Hyacinth muscari* is the small Grape Hyacinth. It is much better at returning each year.

IMPATIENS

Impatiens balsamina
im-PAY-she-enz bal-SAM-eh-nah

Annual · Shade
Ht. 10"-24" Spread 18"-24"
Spacing 9"-12"

HABIT:	Colorful low-spreading annual with tender stems, foliage and flowers. Summer blooms of orange, white, pink, red and purple.
CULTURE:	Plant in well prepared beds in shade after the last frost. Must have excellent drainage.
USES:	Annual beds, pots, hanging baskets. One of the best flowers for shady areas.
PROBLEMS:	Cutworms, red spider mites and slugs.
NOTES:	Native to India and China. 'New Guinea' has showy foliage and can take much more sun. All varieties are very tender to freezing.

IRIS

Iris spp.
EYE-ris

Perennial · Sun
Ht. 10"-40" Spread 3'-4'
Spacing 6"-24"

HABIT:	Vertical leaves, spreads by underground rhizomes, available in any color. Beardless and Bearded are the major groups.
CULTURE:	Iris culture varies greatly — some of the Beardless Irises (Japanese and Louisiana) can grow in or on the edge of water. Others like Siberian need to be continually moist. Others like Tall Bearded need good drainage. When clumps get too thick, dig with turning fork, cut leaves to 6"-8" and replant, placing Bearded Iris rhizomes even with the soil surface and Beardless 1"-2" below the surface.
USES:	Spring flowers, perennial gardens, cut flowers.
PROBLEMS:	None serious.
NOTES:	Iris means rainbow in Greek so I like to plant mixed color masses. Louisianas and Spurias grow the tallest. Intermiates are a good choice for a landscape Iris. Check bibliography for additional information.

LANTANA (Native)

Lantana spp.
lan-TAN-ah

Perennial - Sun
Ht. 1'-3' Spread 2'-4'
Spacing 12"-18"

HABIT: Bushy growth all summer with flowers of yellow, white, orange, pink, blue and purple. Trailing varieties are available. Some of the tough varieties will return each year.
CULTURE: Easy, any well drained soil, likes good bed preparation. Drought tolerant. Regular fertilization will create more blooms.
USES: Summer color, pots, hanging baskets, attracts hummingbirds.
PROBLEMS: Whiteflies but no big deal. Gets woody with age.
NOTES: Berries are poisonous. Plant in spring. Native Texas Lantana is *L. horrida*. Use as an annual in the northern part of the state.

LISIANTHUS (Native)

Eustoma grandiflorum
you-STO-mah liz-ee-AN-thus gran-dee-FLORE-rum

Annual - Sun
Ht. 1'-2' Spread 1½'-3'
Spacing 1'-2'

HABIT: Upright plant, bell shaped flowers in white, pink and blue.
CULTURE: Can take fairly dry well drained soil but likes even moisture better. Does quite well in our heat.
USES: Annual flowers.
PROBLEMS: Few if any.
NOTES: Also called Texas Bluebells. Grows wild in Texas but has been picked almost clean.

LYTHRUM

Lythrum salicaria
LITH-rum sal-eh-CARE-ee-ah

Perennial - Sun/Light Shade
Ht. 2'-4' Spread 3'-4'
Spacing 3'

HABIT: Pink or lavender flowers on terminal spikes. Plant is fairly woody and upright. Mother plants are somewhat invasive — cultivars are not.
CULTURE: Tough and very adaptable. Can grow easily in damp, normal of dry soils of various pH.
USES: Perennial garden, color accent, cutting garden.
PROBLEMS: None.
NOTES: Also called Loosestrife. 'Happy,' 'Morden's Gleam,' 'Firecandle' and 'Morden's Pink' are good cultivars.

MARIGOLD

Tagetes spp.
ta-GET-tes

Annual - Sun
Ht. 1'-2' Spread 1'-2'
Spacing 9"-12"

HABIT: Fast, lacy foliage, yellow or orange flowers. Would last from spring to frost if it wasn't for the red spider.
CULTURE: Any soil, best in well drained full sun location. Will reseed and come up the following year but will be weaker than original plants. Can be planted mid summer for fall flowers.
USES: Summer color, cut flowers, border, mass planting.
PROBLEMS: Red spider, short life.
NOTES: Mexican Mint Marigold is a herb with yellow flowers in late summer. Available in many container sizes. Native to Central America.

NIEREMBERGIA
Nierembergia spp.
near-im-BERG-ee-ah

Perennial - Sun/Part Shade
Ht. 6"-12" Spread 12"-18"
Spacing 9"-12"

HABIT:	Low bunch growth with blue or white flowers in summer.
CULTURE:	Well drained organic soil is best with moderate water and fertilization.
USES:	Colorful border, rock gardens, perennial gardens, stone walls.
PROBLEMS:	Few if any.
NOTES:	Also called Cup Flower. Native to Argentina. Plant from containers in spring or fall.

OXALIS
Oxalis spp.
ox-AL-is

Perennial - Part Shade
Ht. 6"-12" Spread 12"-15"
Spacing 9"-12"

HABIT:	Tough, low growing perennial. Available in several colors. Foliage looks like clover.
CULTURE:	Easy to grow in light to fairly heavy shade. Can grow in full sun but prefers afternoon shade. Normal bed preparation, water and fertilizer.
USES:	Low border, perennial gardens.
PROBLEMS:	Red spider mites.
NOTES:	Also called Wood Sorrell.

PANSY
Viola hybrids
vie-OH-la

Annual - Sun
Ht. 6"-8" Spread 8"-12"
Spacing 6"-9"

HABIT:	Low growing winter and spring flowering annual. Yellow, white, blue and bronze.
CULTURE:	Well prepared and drained beds, ample water and fertilizer.
USES:	Winter and cool season flowers.
PROBLEMS:	Extreme freezes, aphids, cutworms.
NOTES:	Plant in October or late winter. In mild winter pansies will bloom from fall to spring. Giant flower varieties are available. Native to Europe.

PENTA
Pentas lanceolata
PEN-tas lan-see-oh-LAY-tah

Annual - Sun/Part Shade
Ht. 24" Spread 18"-24"
Spacing 12"-18"

HABIT:	Blooms all summer in red, white, lavender, pink and candy stripe.
CULTURE:	Easy to grow annual. Plant after frost danger in well drained soil. Moderate water and fertilizer needs. Best to allow for afternoon shade.
USES:	Summer annual. Great for true red color.
PROBLEMS:	None serious.
NOTES:	Not widely used but should be. Also called Egyptian Star Cluster.

PERIWINKLE

Catharanthus roseus
ca-tha-RAN-thus ro-SAY-us

Annual - Sun
Ht. 9"-12" Spread 12"-15"
Spacing 9"-12"

HABIT:	Low, compact annual for dry areas.
CULTURE:	Plant in any well drained bed in full sun after the weather turns permanently warmer.
USES:	Summer color.
PROBLEMS:	Too much water or planting too early in the spring is sure death for this plant.
NOTES:	Always plant the dwarf varieties so they won't lay over on you. Photo shows most popular 'Bright Eye.' Native to Madagascar. 'Pink Panther' is a new dark pink or light red with white undersides of petals and reddish stems.

PETUNIA

Petunia x *hybrida*
pe-TUNE-ee-ah HI-brid-ah

Annual - Sun
Ht. 12"-24" Spread 18"-24"
Spacing 9"-12"

HABIT:	Tender summer flowering annual. Available in many colors.
CULTURE:	Plant before last frost in well prepared beds with good drainage. Needs high fertilization for best blooms.
USES:	Summer flowers, pots, hanging baskets.
PROBLEMS:	Cutworms, caterpillars and summer heat.
NOTES:	Do not plant as a summer annual. It likes the cool parts of the growing seasons but hates the hot parts. 'Madness' and 'Cherry Blossom' are more heat tolerant. Native to South America. Wild Petunia *(Barleria cristata)* has purple flowers and is perennial.

PLUMBAGO

Plumbago spp.
plum-BAY-go

Perennial - Sun/Part Shade
Ht. 1'-3' Spread 2'-5'
Spacing 12"-18"

HABIT:	Sprawling, fast growing perennial. Blooms in summer blue or white. Dies to ground in fall, returns in spring.
CULTURE:	Likes good beds but is drought tolerant.
USES:	Summer flowers, stone walls, natural settings.
PROBLEMS:	Few if any.
NOTES:	Native to South Africa. *Ceratostigma plumbaginoides* (shown in photo) has dark blue flowers. *P. capensis* has baby blue flowers and is larger growing. *P. auriculata* 'Alba' has white flowers.

POPPY

Papaver spp.
pa-PAY-ver

Annual - Sun
Ht. 12"-4', Spread 12"-3'
Spacing 9"-15"

HABIT:	Annual flower (many colors) but reseeds to return each spring. Lovely flowers on long slender stems. Lacy and hairy foliage. Blooms usually late April to early May. Some varieties will perennialize.
CULTURE:	Plant seeds directly in beds in September. Likes cool weather.
USES:	Spring flowers.
PROBLEMS:	Heat.
NOTES:	Oriental Poppy *(P. orientale)*, Iceland Poppy *(P. nudicaule)*, Corn Poppy *(P. Rhoeas)*, Opium Poppy *(P. somniferum)*. Native to Greece and the Orient.

PORTULACA

Portulaca grandiflora
por-chew-LAC-ah gran-dee-FLORE-ah

Annual - Sun
Ht. 6" Spread 12"-18"
Spacing 9"-12"

HABIT:	Low growing annual with succulent stems and rose-like flowers in summer. Flowers are open in the morning and close during the heat of the day. New flowers every day.
CULTURE:	Easy, any well drained soil. Low water and food requirements.
USES:	Colorful groundcover, summer flowers, pots, hanging baskets.
PROBLEMS:	Afternoon heat closes flowers, snails, slugs and cutworms.
NOTES:	Purslane, a close kin, is probably better since the flowers stay open longer during the day. Native to South America.

PRIMROSE, EVENING (Native)

Oenothera spp.
ee-no-THEE-rhu

Perennial - Sun
Ht. 1'-1½' Spread 2'-3'
Spacing 12"-18"

HABIT:	Sprawling perennial with long lasting showy flower display in the spring. Not a plant for well groomed garden. White or pink flowers.
CULTURE:	Plant from containers in the spring or seeds in the fall.
USES:	Wildflowers in grassy areas, carefree perennial garden.
PROBLEMS:	Ragged looking when not in bloom.
NOTES:	Also called Texas Buttercup. Native from Missouri to Texas. Do not fertilize wild flowers. The small wine-color flower in the photo is another native wildflower called Wine Cup.

ROSE, ANTIQUE

Rosa spp.
ROW-sa

Perennial - Sun
Ht. 12"-12' Spread 24"-8'
Spacing 36"-8'

HABIT:	Old roses vary from big bushes to low groundcovers to large climbing vines. They are better for landscape use than the hybrids because they are prettier plants, more fragrant and much easier to maintain.
CULTURE:	Use lots of organic material and sulphur in the bed preparation. Use the same water and fertilizer program as for your other plantings.
USES:	Vines, perennial color, mass, fragrance, nostalgia, etc.
PROBLEMS:	Black spot, aphids.
NOTES:	Many great choices available. Native worldwide. *Rosa wichuraiana* 'Porteriifolia' is an almost indestructible low-growing, groundcover type rose. 'Cecile Brunner,' 'Betty Prior,' 'Marie Pavie' and 'Elsie Poulsen' are carefree choices. 'Petite Pink Scotch' is a miniature rose that has lovely delicate foliage and forms a symmetrical 3' mound.

ROSEMARY

Rosmarinus officinalis
roz-mah-RINE-us oh-fis-si-NAL-lis

Evergreen - Sun/Part Shade
Ht. 1'-4' Spread 4'
Spacing 12"-18"

HABIT:	Low growing and spreading herb. Leaves resemble thick pine needles. Light blue flowers.
CULTURE:	Likes well drained, slightly alkaline soil. Drought tolerant once established.
USES:	Groundcover, summer flowers, herb for cooking.
PROBLEMS:	Few.
NOTES:	*Rosemary officinalis* 'Arp' is the most cold hearty shrub type Rosemary. 'Lockwood de Forest' and 'Prostratus' are low growing forms. Native to the Mediterranean.

SALVIA, GREGGI (Native)

Salvia greggi
SAL-vee-uh GREG-eye

Perennial - Sun
Ht. 2'-3' Spread 3'-4'
Spacing 2'

HABIT:	Shrubby perennial with red, pink, salmon or white blooms all summer long.
CULTURE:	Any well drained soil, extremely drought tolerant.
USES:	Spring, summer and fall color, perennial gardens.
PROBLEMS:	None.
NOTES:	Also called Autumn Sage. Native to Texas. Annual Salvia likes plenty of water and fertilizer. Scarlet Sage *(S. coccinea)* is a native perennial 1'-2' ht. and looks like the annual Salvia. *S. regla* blooms in the fall; *S. guaranitica* has intense blue flowers, 3'-4' ht. but is not quite as winter hearty as *S. greggi. Salvia leucantha* is a large growing perennial with beautiful foliage and purple flowers in late summer.

SALVIA, MEALY BLUE (Native)

Salvia farinacea
SAL-vee-uh far-eh-NAY-see-ah

Perennial - Sun/Part Shade
Ht. 2'-3' Spread 2'-3'
Spacing 1'-2'

HABIT:	Gray-green foliage and long blue flowers on vertical stems.
CULTURE:	Easy, any well drained soil, drought tolerant, low fertilizer requirements.
USES:	Summer flowers, perennial garden, blue color.
PROBLEMS:	None.
NOTES:	Native to Central and West Texas and New Mexico. Plant in fall or spring. A compact cultivar is now available.

SNAPDRAGON

Antirrhinum spp.
an-TIR-eh-num

Annual - Sun/Part Shade
Ht. 12"-24" Spread 9"-12"
Spacing 9"-12"

HABIT:	Upright flower spikes available in many colors.
CULTURE:	Plant in sun or semi shade. Likes alkaline soil, moderate water and regular fertilization. Likes cool weather.
USES:	Cool season color, cut flowers.
PROBLEMS:	Rust, cutworms.
NOTES:	Plant in late winter or early spring. Native to the Mediterranean.

THRIFT

Phlox subulata
FLOCKS sub-you-LAY-tah

Perennial - Sun
Ht. 6"-8" Spread 10"-12"
Spacing 10"-12"

HABIT:	Low growing and spreading perennial that acts like an evergreen in mild winters. Blooms in spring in pink, blue and white. Hot pink is the most common color.
CULTURE:	Easy, any well drained soil, moderate water and fertilizer needs.
USES:	Dwarf border, spring color, stone walls.
PROBLEMS:	None.
NOTES:	Reliable to bloom year after year. Plant in fall or spring. Native to North America. Also called Moss Phlox. 'Blue Emerald' is the best; its foliage is lush and dark green all summer.

TULIP
Tulip spp.
TOO-lip

Annual - Sun
Ht. 9"-12" Spread 6"-9"
Spacing 6"-9"

HABIT: Flowers on long stems in spring. Dwarf and tall growing varieties available. Single, double and parrot type flowers available. All colors available.
CULTURE: Plant after the weather is good and cold in well prepared and well drained beds. Pull out and throw away after blooming.
USES: Spring color.
PROBLEMS: Expensive, will usually not return in this area — should be replanted each year.
NOTES: Plant in pansy beds for dramatic display in the spring. Can be planted farther apart (12"-18") if planted in this fashion. Native to Asia.

VERBENA
Verbena spp.
ver-BEAN-ah

Perennial - Sun
Ht. 9"-12" Spread 12"-18"
Spacing 9"-12"

HABIT: Low spreading perennial, blooms red, white, salmon, purple all summer.
CULTURE: Easy, well drained beds, low water and fertilization requirements.
USES: Summer color.
PROBLEMS: Red spider mites occasionally.
NOTES: The natives are Prairie Verbena (*V. bipinnatifida*) and Moss Verbena (*V. tenuisecta*). 'Pink Parfait' is a beautiful, large flowered evergreen. The cultivated varieties are good as well.

YARROW
Achillea spp.
ah-KILL-ee-uh

Perennial - Sun
Ht. 2' Spread 2'
Spacing 1'-2'

HABIT: Upright, lacy foliage, flat topped clusters of flowers. Flower colors include white, rose, pink and yellow and red.
CULTURE: Easy in any well drained soil.
USES: Perennial border, cut flowers.
PROBLEMS: Some varieties grow tall and need to be staked.
NOTES: Native to Europe. *Achillea millefolium* is a white blooming, very tough species. Plant in spring or fall.

ZINNIA
Zinnia spp.
ZEN-ee-ah

Annual - Sun
Ht. 8"-36" Spread 12"-24"
Spacing 12"

HABIT: Open upright growth. Flowers of all colors and sizes on long stems in summer. Easy to grow from seed.
CULTURE: Any loose soil, fairly drought tolerant. Add supersphosphate for more blooms.
USES: Summer flowers, cut flowers.
PROBLEMS: Mildew, cutworms, red spider mites. Gets ragged toward the end of summer.
NOTES: Native to Mexico and Central America. Plant from seeds or pots in spring.

DEFINITIONS OF TERMS

Acid, Alkaline — Descriptions of soil or water pH, 7 being neutral. A pH above 7 indicates alkalinity, and a pH less than 7 indicates acidity.

Aerate — Punch holes in, or loosen soil in order to allow better air circulation.

Annual — Plants which reach maturity in one growing season. The seed germinates, the plant grows, blooms, seeds and dies within a year or less. Plants that have to be replanted each year are also referred to as annuals (e.g. Marigolds).

Aphids — Small insects of assorted sizes and colors, usually oval in shape, that damage plants by sucking plant juices.

Asps — Hairy caterpillars found in trees and shrubs in the fall. These pests have a very toxic sting. A non-toxic treatment that kills caterpillars is Bacillus thuringiensis, also called BT. BT is a bacterial parasite that sells under the brand names Dipel, Attack, Thuricide, Bactisphere and Biotrol.

Bagworms — Insects that build bag-like cocoons on conifers and other plants.

Balanced Fertilizer — A fertilizer that contains, in equal or nearly equal proportion, some measure of the three primary fertilizing elements: nitrogen (N), phosphorous (P), and potassium (K).

Balled and Burlapped (B & B) — A method of packaging plants and trees with a ball of soil around the roots, wrapped in burlap.

Bare Root — A method of packaging dormant plants having no soil around the roots.

Biennial — A description of the life cycle of certain plants which require two years to produce seed.

Black Spot — Leaf and stem fungus that primarily attacks roses.

Bonsai — Japanese meaning "to cultivate in a tray." An Oriental art of growing dwarfed, carefully trained miniature plants. The purpose is to create a tree or landscape in miniature.

Borers — Very damaging insects whose larvae bore holes in trees.

Border Planting — Any plant or group of plants which act as a barrier or boundary to segregate sections of a property.

Bract — Leaf-like plant part, sometimes colorful, located below the flower or on the stalk of a flower cluster.

Bulb — Any plant that grows from a thickened underground structure. A true bulb is more or less rounded and composed of fleshy scales that store food.

Caliche — A rock-like deposit of calcium carbonate (lime) beneath the soil surface This condition is found in the dry areas of the Southwest.

Cambium — A thin layer of tissue producing cells between the bark and the sapwood of a woody plant.

Caterpillars and Worms — Pests that come in hundreds of varieties. Most are moth and butterfly larvae that feed on foliage.

Chlorosis — The yellowing of leaves (especially between the leaf veins) caused by the lack of iron or other nutrients.

Complete Fertilizer — A plant food containing the three primary elements: nitrogen, phosphorous and potassium.

Compost — Organic matter that has been decomposed by a process of fermentation. An excellent soil conditioner, compost is also a mild fertilizer.

Conifer — A plant that produces seeds in cones and is usually evergreen. Their leaves may be needlelike (e.g. Pines) or scale-like (e.g. Junipers).

Cool Season Grasses — Grasses that natively grow in cool climates, used here in shade areas and for winter overseeding (e.g. Ryegrass, Bent, Fescue, *Poa trivialis*).

Corm — Like a bulb; thickened underground vertical stem which produces roots, leaves and flowers during the growing season. It differs from a bulb in that food is stored in the solid center tissue, whereas food is stored in scales of bulbs.

Crown Gall — A bacterial disease causing deformation at the base of plants at the ground line; especially prevalent on conifers and members of the rose family.

Cultivar — A horticultural variety that has originated under cultivation. Cultivar names are now formed from not more than three words and usually distinguished typographically by the use of single quotation marks, 'Early Black.'

Cultivate — (1) To grow or plant domestically. (2) To hoe or dig around a live plant for the purpose of eliminating weeds and breaking up crusty soil.

Cutworms — Night feeding worms that are particularly destructive to tender bedding plants.

Deciduous — Foliage drops in fall and returns in the spring.

Desiccation — Drying out and dying.

Diatomaceous Earth (D-Earth) — The skeletal remains (silica compounds and trace minerals) of diatoms — single celled aquatic algae. An effective insecticide that works by the microscopic particles cutting an insect's waxy outer coat destroying its moisture balance.

Dioecious — Male and female flowers on different plants.

Division — Cutting or dividing root clumps and replanting.

Dormant — A period of time that a plant is not growing, normally winter.

Dwarf — A plant whose size has been reduced, either by nature or by vegetative means, such as grafting or budding onto a dwarfing understock. Many annuals have been hybridized to produce dwarf forms from seed.

Earwigs — Long, thin, beetle-like insects that stink when you step on them, and feed on flowers, other insects and decaying organic matter.

Espalier — Shrubs or trees trimmed and trained to grow flat against a wall, fence, trellis, wire, etc., in a pattern or mass.

Evergreen — Foliage stays green all year and never loses all the leaves at one time.

Family — Groups of plants that share similar characteristics.

Fertilizer — Any plant food.

Water Soluble Fertilizer — Fertilizer that is mixed with water before applying.

Fireblight — A disease that strikes pyracantha, loquat and other members of the rose family. It is characterized by the burned look of the tip growth.

Foliar Feeding — The application of fertilizer by spraying the leaves of a plant with a mild liquid fertilizer solution.

Forcing — Hastening a plant to the flowering or fruiting stage out of its normal season; usually done by growing under controlled conditions indoors.

Foundation Planting — Growing plants along the foundation of a building.

Friable — Loose and crumbly soil that permits air circulation and water drainage.

Gall — A rounded swelling on a leaf, twig or stem of a plant, usually caused by fungi or insect stings.

Genus — A further breakdown (subcategory) of the family category of plants. The genus to which a plant belongs is the first word in a plant's botanical name.

Germination — Earliest stage of the formation of a plant from seed.

Green Lacewing — A beneficial aphid eating insect.

Groundcover — Speading plants that cover bare ground.

Hardening Off — The process of slowly changing a plant's light, temperature, water or fertilization to prepare it for a change in weather or location.

Herbaceous — With the texture of a herb as opposed to a woody texture.

Herbicide — A chemical applied to the soil to control weeds. Selective herbicides kill only specific plants while leaving surrounding vegetation unharmed; non-selective herbicides kill all vegetation in the area to which they are applied.

Humus — The last stages of decomposition of animal or vegetable matter into a soft brown or black substance.

Hybrid — A plant resulting from the cross of two species.

Iron Chelate — A combination of iron and a complex organic substance that assists in making iron readily available to roots of plants. Used to cure chlorosis.

June Bugs — Insects whose larvae are grub worms that do great damage to lawns.

Lacebugs — Insects that are particularly bad on pyracantha.

Ladybug — Also called Ladybird Beetle. The best friendly insect that feeds on aphids and other small insect pests.

Leafhoppers — Small insects with piercing-sucking mouthparts. These pests usually suck plant juices from the undersides of leaves.

Leaf Miners — The larvae of various kinds of moths, midges and flies. They feed inside the plant between the leaf surfaces and create serpentine trails or ugly blotches on the leaf.

Loam — Soil consisting of sand and light clay particles. Usually fairly big in organic material.

Mealybugs — White fuzzy insects closely related to scale. They may appear singly or in groups on branches or twigs.

Spider Mites — Tiny pests which cause damage by sucking sap from lower leaf surfaces. Normally referred to as red spider. Webs will appear when the plant is under heavy infestation. Very hard to control.

Monoecious — Male and female flowers on the same plant.

Mulch — Material placed on top of the soil which serves to reduce or prevent weed growth, insulate soil from drastic temperature changes, reduce moisture loss and enhance the appearance of the bed. Peat moss, compost, bark, sawdust, straw and leaves are examples of mulch.

N-P-K — Symbols for nitrogen, phosphorus and potassium.

Naturalize — Random planting or spreading. When plants are allowed to reseed themselves and grow as wildflowers, they have the ability to naturalize.

Naturalizing — The reverse of plant domestication. A naturalized plant is one that has "escaped" from the garden and grows wild, propagating itself. Plants are naturalized intentionally or by accident, as when the wind or animals transport the seed.

Nematodes — Microscopic worm-like organisms that attack the root systems of certain plants. Very hard to control. Some feed on insects and are beneficial.

Organic Fertilizer — A fertilizer made from previously living matter or from animal waste. Common organic fertilizers include cottonseed meal, bone meal, dried blood, sewage sludge and animal manure.

Organic Material — Any material that can be incorporated into the soil to improve its condition and was at one time a living substance. Peat moss, bark, compost and manure are examples.

Ornamental Tree — Small sized tree used more for decorativ purposes than for shade. Normally used for color (flowers or colorful foliage) or for small areas or courtyards.

Peat Moss — The partially decomposed remains of several different mosses. It is a spongy, organic soil additive which is highly water retentive and very acidic.

Perennial — Usually means a plant of which the top portion dies each winter and regrows the following spring; however, some keep their leaves year round.

Perlite — Mineral used in container-soil mixes. It is very lightweight, white, porous, granular and used for loosening and allowing more air into the soil.

pH — Symbol describing the acidity or alkalinity of soil or water, 7 being neutral, less than 7 being acid, greater than 7 being alkaline.

Pick Pruning — Selectively removing limbs and branches rather than shearing.

Pleaching — The interweaving and plaiting together of plant branches. After this training method, subsequent pruning maintains a neat, somewhat floral pattern.

Pyrethrum — A natural insecticide derived from the Pyrethrum flower, a variety of chrysanthemum.

Rhizome — A long and slender, or thick and fleshy stem which grows horizontally along or under the soil.

Scale — Insect pests which are divided into armored and soft groups. Waxy secretions and hard skins cover the armored group. Soft scales usually secrete a substance which causes blackening of foliage and sticky film on cars, walks, etc.

Scarify — Plow-like scratching or breaking up of the surface of the soil in order to loosen or aerate. Also refers to the treatment given to hard seeds to hasten germination.

Seedling — A young plant grown from seed.

Shade Tree — Large growing trees that provide a canopy top that allows other planting or activity to take place beneath.

Sharp Sand — Washed sand, which is considered organic-matter free, used to make concrete, and used in planting bed preparation.

Shrub — A multiple-stemmed, usually small woody plant with an upright habit of growth.

Snails and Slugs — Found where the ground is consistently moist. These pests inhabit groundcover plantings where they hide during the day and feed on plants at night.

Soil Test — An analysis of the fertilizing elements contained in the soil. Such a test is usually performed by a state department of soil conservation, but soil test kits are available commercially.

Sphagnum — A moss native to swamp conditions. These mosses are used in air layering and for lining hanging baskets.

Red Spider — Tiny pests which cause damage by sucking sap (from lower leaf surfaces). Actually mites, not spiders. Webs will appear when the plant is under heavy infestation. Very hard to control.

Spp. — A symbol used with botanical names after the genus to indicate that there are many different species of that particular kind of plant.

Stolon — A vinelike stem that grows along the ground or just under the surface and produces a new plant at its tip.

Succulent — A plant that is drought tolerant due to its ability to store water in its fleshy foliage.

Sucker — A weak shoot that grows quickly from the base of a plant or from the joint of two normal limbs.

Taproot — A main root which grows straight down. In dry areas some taproots grow very deep to reach a moisture source.

Tendrils — Threadlike projections found on some vines which enable them to climb and cling to supports.

Topsoil — The uppermost layer of soil.

Tree — A large upright woody plant.

Tuber — A short, thickened underground stem or root.

Tuberous Root — A underground food storage structure with buds at the upper end of the root. Example is Dahlia.

Understory Tree — Small to medium size tree planted under the canopy of larger trees.

Variegated Foliage — Foliage that is striped, blotched, or edged with some color other than green.

Variety — The subdivision of a species; a group of individual plants within a species which are distinct in form or minor characteristics usually perpetuated through generations by seed.

Vermiculite — A heated and puffed-up mineral which forms spongelike, lightweight granules useful to add to container soil.

Vine — A long-stemmed plant that trails over the ground, or climbs if support is provided. Some vines climb by twining or by tendrils that cling to the support. Other vines must be tied to their support.

Wettable Powder — A finely-ground chemical which can be mixed into water and sprayed onto plants.

Whiteflies — Small, snow-white insects which are usually found in large numbers. Whitefly nymphs suck juices from the underside of leaves, damaging the plant.

Woody — Characterized by a woodlike texture as opposed to an herblike texture.

INDEX

INDEX